SHAMANS AND ROBOTS

A UNIVOCAL BOOK

Drew Burk, Consulting Editor

Univocal Publishing was founded by Jason Wagner and Drew Burk as an independent publishing house specializing in artisanal editions and translations of texts spanning the areas of cultural theory, media archaeology, continental philosophy, aesthetics, anthropology, and more. In 2017, Univocal ceased operations as an independent publishing house and became a series with its publishing partner, the University of Minnesota Press.

Univocal authors include:

Miguel Abensour	Sylvère Lotringer
Judith Balso	Jean Malaurie
Roger Bartra	Michael Marder
Jean Baudrillard	Serge Margel
Philippe Beck	Quentin Meillassoux
Simon Critchley	Friedrich Nietzsche
Fernand Deligny	Peter Pál Pelbart
Jacques Derrida	Jacques Rancière
Vinciane Despret	Lionel Ruffel
Georges Didi-Huberman	Felwine Sarr
Jean Epstein	Michel Serres
Vilém Flusser	Gilbert Simondon
Barbara Glowczewski	Étienne Souriau
Évelyne Grossman	Isabelle Stengers
Félix Guattari	Sylvain Tesson
Olivier Haralambon	Eugene Thacker
David Lapoujade	Antoine Volodine
François Laruelle	Elisabeth von Samsonow
David Link	Siegfried Zielinski

SHAMANS AND ROBOTS

On Ritual, the Placebo Effect, and
Artificial Consciousness

ROGER BARTRA

TRANSLATED BY GUSTI GOULD

A UNIVOCAL BOOK

University of Minnesota Press
Minneapolis
London

First published as *Chamanes y robots* by Editorial Anagrama, Barcelona, 2019. Copyright 2019 by Roger Bartra.

English translation copyright 2024 by Roger Bartra

All rights reserved. No part of this publication may be reproduced, stored in a retrieval system, utilized for purposes of training artificial intelligence technologies, or transmitted in any form or by any means, electronic, mechanical, photocopying, recording, or otherwise, without the prior written permission of the publisher.

Published by the University of Minnesota Press
111 Third Avenue South, Suite 290
Minneapolis, MN 55401-2520
http://www.upress.umn.edu

ISBN 978-1-5179-1749-4 (pb)

A Cataloging-in-Publication record for this book is available from the Library of Congress.

Printed in the United States of America on acid-free paper

The University of Minnesota is an equal-opportunity educator and employer.

UMP BmB 2024

CONTENTS

Prologue   vii

PART I. THE RITUALS OF PLEASURE AND THE WORD: ANTHROPOLOGY OF THE PLACEBO EFFECT

1 The Placebo   3
2 The Ligatures of Qusta ibn Luqa   9
3 The Magical Powers   17
4 A Shamanic Journey in Search of the Lost Soul   27
5 Neurology of the Placebo Effect   33
6 On Electronic Amulets and Catharsis   43
7 Zombies and Transhumanists   51

PART II. THE CONSTRUCTION OF AN ARTIFICIAL CONSCIOUSNESS: ANTHROPOLOGY OF THE ROBOTIC EFFECT

8 The Mystery of Thinking Machines   61
9 The Robotic Effect   69

10 How Do You Educate a Robot?   75

11 Panpsychism   87

12 A Mechanical Consciousness   93

13 Robotic Culture   97

14 Prostheses and Symbols   103

15 Robotic Experiences   109

16 Emancipation of the Exocerebrums   115

17 Sentimental Machines   125

18 Proof of the Placebo   135

Notes   *143*

PROLOGUE

The massive expansion of artificial intelligence will eliminate thousands of jobs in the near future; human workers are already being replaced by robots that perform tasks faster and more efficiently. We are experiencing a profound technological revolution. There is a generalized fear that these intelligent machines will acquire higher forms of consciousness and even be able to absorb human minds that will function with artificial supports and no biological bodies. There are those who even hope that this robotic future will lead to the creation of new forms of human life, freed from the confines of a biological condition. In reality, humans have always relied on artificial prostheses that have extraordinarily expanded the biological limits of consciousness, but today we are witnessing an accelerated development of sophisticated machines that possess artificial intelligence.

In this book I explore the extension of the functions of consciousness into the cultural networks that humans have woven, and I do so by focusing on the way in which rituals influence cerebral textures. I examine shamanic rites, describing their ancient or traditional expressions, as well as their forms in modern medicine. At the core of these rituals is a phenomenon that has been increasingly recognized and studied: the so-called placebo effect. It involves a close functional relation between cultural devices and the biological operations of the central nervous system. This phenomenon can provide us with important insights into the part of the human mind connected to the artificial nature of rituals and cultural prostheses. These are precisely the keys whose components engineers strive to decipher in their attempt to make robots function with consciousness structures similar to those of humans. And so we will find a certain parallelism between the processes triggered by a shaman or a physician in the mind of the patient who wants to be healed, and the mechanisms an engineer constructs to give a robot something akin to consciousness. In both cases, there is a link between artificial processes and conscious behaviors. If robots are going to be conscious, they must be built as mixed systems, resembling the hybrid character of human consciousness.

Two conditions tie the shamanic and robotic phenomena together: suffering and pleasure. The healing rituals of both doctors and shamans seek to reduce or eliminate human pain and suffering, and in their place, provide pleasure and well-being. In principle, artificial intelligence and robots are constructed for the purpose of reducing the fatigue and distress that afflict humans in the workplace. Work, like disease, is a source of pain and penury. I am not saying that work is a disease, but both are certainly conditions that produce suffering. The problem confronting the builders of robots is that their machines lack sensitivity, and this deficiency apparently hinders the ability of consciousness to exist. And so, we are facing a paradox:

consciousness is sustained in suffering, but humans are determined to alleviate it, and even eliminate it. Today's robots are insensitive machines that do not suffer, and thus appear incapable of possessing consciousness.

The other dimension of emotions and feelings that is connected with the exploration of consciousness is pleasure. Many of the prostheses that extend consciousness into the social spheres are conceived to satisfy, alleviate, and please. The placebo effect, which I discuss in the first part of this book, directly refers to the way in which pleasure, as well as alleviation, is provided to humans. At the end of the eighteenth century, the medical literature began to recognize the placebo as a medication administered to the patient more to provide pleasure than to be of actual benefit. Further ahead, the reader will begin to see that pleasure per se can be a benefit, even if the substance prescribed to the patient is innocuous. However, as I describe in the second part of this book, pleasure and emotions are completely foreign to the robots we currently know. What significance can this insensitive condition have for those dedicated to building artificial intelligence and attempting to provide machines with artificial consciousness? In the pages ahead I will begin to explore some of the artificial dimensions of consciousness that I did not cover in my book *Anthropology of the Brain*: the placebo effect and the consciousness of robots.[1] I believe they are very significant aspects to be contemplated and can contribute to understanding the mystery of human consciousness.

There are those who are convinced that consciousness is a mere illusion resulting from the functioning of our brain, and thus there is no mystery to investigate. Consciousness would be a kind of trick produced by neuronal activity. In contrast, from the perspective of panpsychism, there are those who believe that consciousness pervades the entire universe and that its expression in humans is only a complex variation of a cosmic phenomenon. Others postulate that consciousness is a fundamental force, similar to gravity. There are theories that attempt to be more reality-based and suggest that consciousness is a quantic phenomenon or a physical process whose nature we still do not understand. In that same line, consciousness is thought to be an emergent physical phenomenon that causes a leap to a highly complex form. And of course, the religious explanation of consciousness is the most extensive, and considers consciousness a spiritual and metaphysical entity.

It is my opinion that consciousness is a singular hybrid phenomenon, characteristic of humans. More precisely, I would say it is a consciousness of self. It is the union of two spheres, the cerebral and the cultural, each of which responds to different laws and whose confluence is still a poorly explained phenomenon. My proposal immediately runs into a problem: two scientific expressions come together here that respond to very different realities: neurology and anthropology. These two scientific spheres—the natural sciences and the social sciences—have long nurtured a mutual distrust.

The intrusions of biology upon sociology have not produced very fruitful results and have been met with a certain rejection by those who study social and cultural phenomena. At the same time, researchers from the hard sciences, such as physics, chemistry, and biology, tend to doubt the scientific character of anthropology and sociology. The abyss separating the natural sciences from the social sciences is deeper than the one separating quantum physics and gravitational physics. As C. P. Snow reminds us, we are still victims of the age-old segregation that separated scientific culture from the humanities.

As such, the reader of this book will quickly realize that the topics addressed require a dimensional convergence of the biological with the cultural. And when the robotic question is added, we are faced with the complication of connecting cybernetic mechanics with the biological and social dimensions. Today, very few persons appear to recognize the need to work on unifying and coordinating scientific domains that are apparently so far apart from each other. And these are the difficulties that provide this book with its essayistic character of a search into territories replete with paradoxes.

Part I
THE RITUALS OF PLEASURE AND THE WORD
ANTHROPOLOGY OF THE PLACEBO EFFECT

1 THE PLACEBO

I wish to invite the reader on a journey that ventures into thorny but intellectually stimulating territories, and which I hope will also be enjoyable. The road ahead is risky and at times tortuous, taking us through the ideas of a ninth-century Arabian physician, the artificial lamentations of medieval mourners who were hired to weep for the dead, and leading to the shamanism of the Lengua Indians of the Paraguayan Chaco. The adventures will continue, reaching the Kuna medicinal healers of Panama, studied by anthropologists, and the psychoanalytic rituals directed at curing schizophrenia, to then discuss neurological studies on the placebo effect. We will also arrive at a brief discussion on catharsis, modern electronic amulets, and transhumanism.

And what do I propose on this trip? I am searching for evidence on the necessity of breaking out of the cranial cage surrounding the brain in order to truly understand the phenomenon of human consciousness. It is an anthropological expedition that explores a perturbing topic: the so-called placebo effect. I first became interested in the theme of consciousness many years ago, and the search led me to write a book, *Anthropology of the Brain,* which originally appeared in Spanish in 2006 and then in English in 2014. But soon after its publication I realized I had not examined a phenomenon that provides evidence supporting my interpretations regarding the links of the brain to its social and cultural environment: the placebo. In the course of my research I have come up against great resistance by neuroscientists who do not accept the idea that consciousness can be partially located outside of the brain, in the symbolic networks of society. They believe that consciousness cannot be a phenomenon that is external to the brain and do not accept that it can have an influence on neuronal activity.

The idea that human consciousness is incapable of influencing the functioning of the brain arises from the affirmation of a basic scientific principle: the physical world is causally closed and therefore no spiritual or metaphysical entity can interfere in the operations of the central nervous system. Many neuroscientists view with suspicion the study of psychosomatic conditions involving an interaction between the body and the mind, when the mind is assumed to be a metaphysical phenomenon. An important point of departure is the idea expressed in the well-known assertion of T. H. Huxley, the great English biologist of the nineteenth century, that the somatic space is closed. In keeping with that affirmation, consciousness is a collateral effect of the functioning of the body that is not capable of influencing somatic processes. According to Huxley, humans are conscious automata. Consciousness would be an epiphenomenon, similar to the whistle of a locomotive or the shadow following the passerby on a sunny day, phenomena that have no influence on the movement of the train or the person's walking. Such an understanding of consciousness is still very widespread among neuroscientists. A simplistic and reductionist explanation of the problem of consciousness is often added to that idea: it would be a phenomenon or process that takes place completely inside the brain, having no extrabiological base.

I criticized that interpretation when I developed the idea that consciousness includes a type of symbolic prosthesis that, in the cultural spaces, prolongs certain functions of the neural networks. This prosthesis, which I have defined as an exocerebrum, is primarily composed of speech, art, music, artificial memories, and different symbolic structures. A very important part of my theory lies in the asseveration that the exocerebral elements of consciousness have a causal power and are capable of modifying and modulating the operation and functions of the neural networks. These exocerebral circuits are not metaphysical recourses and are not found outside of the causal closure within which scientists correctly circumscribe their explanations.

To sustain this assertion I have embarked on the exploration of the strange and fascinating process that physicians call the placebo effect. This effect is very real and provides demonstrable evidence that the symbolic structures rooted in culture are capable of influencing cerebral functions through consciousness. Scientific studies show that the use of pharmacologically innocuous substances, as well as the performance of sham operations, have demonstrable somatic repercussions. The key to the placebo effect is found in the fact that the patient firmly believes that the remedy a physician (or a shaman) applies is efficient. The placebo has been shown to produce observable physiological effects, such as changes in blood pressure, heart rate, and gastric activity; it even leaves signals in the neural networks. Placebos have been successfully used in the treatment of pain, anxiety, depression, ulcers, skin diseases, rheumatoid arthritis, asthma, high blood pressure, autoimmune diseases, and Parkinson's disease. The nocebo effect, which is the opposite of the placebo effect, has not been as widely studied.

To begin my reflections, I would like to explore a significant medieval antecedent regarding the medicinal use of the placebo effect. It concerns the text of a Syrian physician who lived approximately from 820 to 910 C.E. Obviously, that medieval doctor did not use the word *placebo*. The term originated as the result of an error made by Saint Jerome when translating verse 9 of Psalm 116 from Hebrew to Latin. Instead of translating "I will walk in the presence of the Lord in the land of the living," he wrote, "I shall please the Lord in the land of the living" (*Placebo Domino in regione vivorum*). As a consequence of that translation error, during the Middle Ages the professional mourners engaged by families to weep for their dead frequently began their artificial lament with verse 9 of Psalm 116. Here, "artificial" weeping became a substitute for "real" weeping. The mourners hired to open the Vespers of the Office of the Dead with their factitious wailing often began the laments reciting that same verse in Latin. As a result, those professional mourners were called "placebos," which led to the word coming to mean "flatterer." Later, the term was utilized to refer to the fake medication prescribed to please the patient. "Placebo" ended up alluding to something "artificial" that was believed to be "real." The essential element is the belief or the faith in an act that is inscribed in the ritual performed by a witch doctor, priest, or physician, who, with the gift of the word and simulation, produces healing and pleasing effects.

Thus, from its very origin the idea of placebo was tied to a ritual whose goal was to reduce the misery caused by adversity, such as the death of a loved one or the distress resulting from disease. The ritual attempted to bestow pleasure and relief upon persons enduring injury or pain. And so the error of Saint Jerome connects us to the need to provide pleasure to, to please, those who suffer. The placebo effect is inscribed in the rituals of pleasure, supported by the immense power of the spoken word. However, unlike the desire of Saint Jerome, the purpose of the rituals is not to please a divine being but to provide humans with relief from their ills. Freud would have liked to think that the placebo rituals are tied to the "pleasure principle," to the emotional processes that motivate persons to seek gratification. Those processes are only repressed by the "reality principle," which postpones or even renounces the gratification, to avoid dangers.[1]

2 THE LIGATURES OF QUSTA IBN LUQA

The ninth-century Syrian physician whom I wish to refer to is Qusta ibn Luqa al-Ba'labakki, which is translated as Constantine, son of Luke, who came from Baalbek. The Syrian city where he was born, around the year 820, was known as Heliopolis during the Roman era. Today it is in Lebanon, about eighty kilometers east of Beirut and some fifty-four kilometers north of Damascus. Qusta was a Christian Melkite of Greek origin, and his writings in Arabic were very important in the transmission of Greek knowledge to the Arab world.[1] He lived in Baghdad for many years and died in Armenia around 910. The influence on the West of this Arab physician, philosopher, astronomer, musician, and mathematician can be confirmed by the fact that one of his books, *On the Difference between Spirit and Soul* (or pneuma and psyche), was one of the few texts not written by Aristotle included in the reading list prepared by the masters at the School of the Arts in Paris in 1254 as part of the study of natural philosophy. He translated many scientific treatises from Greek to Arabic and was the author of dozens of works.[2]

A Christian, Qusta wrote a medical guide for those making

the pilgrimage to Mecca (*Risāla Fī Tadbīr Safar Al-ḥaǧǧ*), in which he recommends the best diet for the traveler and describes the possible illnesses that can afflict the pilgrim on the road, as well as their treatments. He refers to fatigue, earache, bronchial diseases, dracunculiasis (Guinea worm disease), insect bites, and problems caused by dust.

Qusta wrote a brief treatise in Arabic, of which only the Latin translation has survived, titled *Physical Ligatures, or On Incantations, Adjurations, and Suspensions around the Neck (De phisicis ligaturi [De incantatione adiuratione colli suspensione])*.[3] There are no known surviving manuscripts in the original Arabic and only fifteen in the Latin version, the oldest of which dates back to the twelfth century. It circulated in printed form as part of a compilation of authors that also included Constantine the African, Galen, Arnau de Vilanova, and Cornelius Agrippa, and generally appeared with the title *De incantatione*. It is the first known medical treatise to recognize the placebo effect and to be open to new perspectives in the treatment of mental illnesses. The text is in the form of a letter to his son, who asked him if the incantations, charms, and amulets worn around the neck were effective as cures and if their healing properties were explained in the Greek texts, as they were in the books from India.

Qusta must have been well versed in Hindu medicine, which greatly influenced the medical practices of the Baghdad of his era. Of course, the medicine practiced in India was highly complex and sophisticated and in no way reduced to the use of charms and amulets. There were even Hindu physicians practicing in Baghdad, and classic Hindu medical texts were translated into Arabic. Manka, a celebrated Hindu physician who lived in the court of Harun al-Rashid, translated medical texts from Sanskrit.

The text of *Physical Ligatures* begins by sustaining the fact that the ancients "seem to have been in agreement in this: the complexion of the body follows the power of the soul" and if the soul is in a state of equilibrium "the action of the body will be equally perfect." But Qusta warns that if the constitution of the body is out of balance, the soul will also be imperfect. "Thus, the powers of the actions of the soul are seen to be imperfect most of the time in children, old people and women," establishing that "the complexion of their body is likewise confirmed to be imperfect as well, and this imperfection similarly affects inhabitants of intemperate regions—as one might expect, the heat of Ethiopia and cold in Scotland."[4] He then concludes that an incantation can be of help if the person believes in it, given that the constitution of the body follows that of the soul: "and this is proved," he says, "by the fact that from fear, sadness, joy, and bewilderment, the body is not only changed in color but also in other ways, such as diarrhea or constipation or excessive weakness." And he adds: "Moreover, I have seen these things to be the causes of protracted alteration of health, particularly on those alterations which will harm minds."

In this context, the reference Qusta makes to Plato is very significant. He says that, according to Plato, when understanding is firm, even if the natural manner is not healthy, an object may be useful, thanks to the intentions of the mind. Thus, if a person believes in an incantation, it can be of help, and to that extent, anything, no matter what it is, can help. Qusta is referring to the *Charmides* dialogue, in which Socrates prescribes a remedy to Charmides, an attractive and intelligent young man, for his headaches. He tells him he should take a certain herb (*phármakon*), but that it is necessary to add some magical words (*epōidós*), a charm that Socrates learned from a Thracian physician, disciple of Zalmoxis, a god that promised immortality to his devotees.[5] Socrates advises Charmides: "And the soul, my good friend, is treated by means of certain charms or incantations, and these incantations are beautiful [or fine] discourses. Temperance derives from such discourses and is engendered in the soul, and once it has been engendered and is present, one can easily supply health to the head and to the rest of the body as well."

It is healing through the power of words, and Qusta invokes it, following the examples of the Indian physicians who firmly believe that charms and incantations are useful. He adds a reference to Hippocrates made by Galen: "If one will say that when the humors of the body are changed the action of the soul is likewise changed, it does not mislead [to say] that the changed action of the soul changes those same [humors]." Thus, yellow bile (choler) increases knowledge and the intellect; black bile (melancholy) induces continence and the inclination to study; blood prompts the desire to talk and walk; phlegm, in contrast, does not affect the soul. Consequently, Qusta believes the inverse is derived from that principle. The physician heals the soul through an incantation, charm, or an amulet worn about the neck, and in turn, the body is also healed.

Qusta proceeds to give several examples. The first is the case of an important nobleman who tells the Syrian doctor that there is a ligature restraining his penis and blocking sexual pleasure. He was referring to an invisible thread that, through witchcraft or a diabolic spell, made men impotent. The challenge was to change the nobleman's thinking and induce him to believe in a remedy. The nobleman stubbornly resisted changing his mind about the problem until Qusta read him a paragraph from the *Book of Cleopatra*. He refers to the *Cosmetica,* a book attributed to Cleopatra that is known only through citations because the text has not survived. "I read the passage," says the Syrian physician, "where it says that one so ligated should take raven's gall mixed with sesame oil and apply it by smearing it all over the body. Upon hearing that, he had confidence in the words of the book and did it, and as soon as he was delivered [from the ligature], his desire for intercourse increased."

He then goes on to describe the examples of objects suspended from the neck, for healing purposes. He cites cases in which Aristotle speaks of the healing power of gems worn around the neck, such as emeralds, which protect against epilepsy; sapphires, which drive the plague away; and sard, which prevents nightmares. In contrast, onyx worn about the neck induces fighting and causes bad dreams.

He writes that Galen recommended wearing a bag containing the excrement from a wolf that had eaten sheep's bones. Dioscorides had a remedy for epilepsy: when the moon is waxing, one should cut open the belly of a young swallow belonging to a first brood, and inside will be two stones, one of a single color and the other multicolored. They should both be placed in a calfskin bag to wear around the neck. Dioscorides also recommended wearing a wild goat's eye tied with sweet marjoram roots to increase sexual desire, and that wearing the finger of an aborted child around the neck would keep the female partner from becoming pregnant. In a similar fashion, Indian physicians recommended placing elephant feces mixed with agave nectar in the woman's vulva to permanently prevent pregnancy.

Qusta states that he had not tried out the remedies suggested by the ancient Greeks or those recommended in the Vedic medicine of India, but he did not deny their efficacy. A Greek physician from the second century C.E., Soranus of Ephesus, whose work Qusta was most certainly familiar with, had already addressed the theme of magical amulets, stating that even though they had no direct effect, he did not oppose their use, because they made the patient happy. Soranus was known for his treatises on women's diseases, and accepted magic and superstition to gain his patients' trust, but he did not believe they had any influence on the course of the disorders. In contrast, Qusta's innovation was his assertion that if patients had faith in the magical objects and charms, they would produce a healthy effect on their bodies. In other words, he recognized the power of suggestion and persuasion.

Inspired by Plato, Qusta ends his text by stating that an excess of rationality on the part of physicians hinders the understanding of many diseases, because they concentrate only on the body and forget the combination that includes the mind. "In some cases," he says, "certain substances have a property incomprehensible to reason because of their subtlety and exactness not [supplied to] the senses because of their [great] profundity." In other words, reason alone cannot penetrate the essence of certain things. Among the incomprehensible things, says Qusta, is the action of a magnet attracting iron; lead that breaks the diamond, something that iron cannot do; caustic soda (sodium hydroxide) that cannot be burned by fire; and the fact that touching certain fish causes a loss of consciousness (he is referring to an electric ray or electric eel). We know these things because of their properties, not because of reasons that enable us to understand their essence. Thus, says Qusta, "something suspended about the neck helps with its property not because of its internal nature, not that I can deny that it can occur, but because of the strengthening of the mind." Namely, their hidden properties are known only through their effects. I believe this is an ancient explanation of the way in which certain symbolic prostheses (special objects worn about the neck, amulets, and charms) adapt to the functioning of the neural networks, and as a result, effects on the body are produced. Such is the nature of the placebo effect. In fact, it is quite possible, as has been described, that a large part of the medical treatments employed before the modern era were actually examples of the placebo effect. Qusta's explanation is not included in the models of academic medicine, even though his text was widely circulated in the West, which is symptomatic of the fact that it was not until the mid-twentieth century that the importance of the placebo effect began to be recognized in medicine.

Reading the explanations of Qusta, we may well be amazed by their similarity to the processes described by today's physicians. Of course, doctors do not presently speak of the influence of magical rituals and charms on the balance of the four humors of Hippocrates. But regarding the placebo effect, they most certainly recognize the influence of the sociocultural and symbolic environment on the flows of endorphins and dopamine in the human body. At the same time, in today's modern societies there are still popular beliefs in the power all kinds of magnetic necklaces and wristbands have on health. Such is the case of the famous Nikken bracelets, Power Balance wristbands, and titanium or negative ion necklaces, which supposedly emit healing vibrations. Devotional scapulars that function as a talisman or amulet, so common in the popular Catholic imaginary, must also be included. Whether innocuous pills or energy-filled necklaces, they are prostheses with the power to heal, and are manipulated by physicians, as well as by quacks, thanks to the power of the spoken word.

Qusta's text emphasizes the importance of manipulating the soul to heal the body. He attempts to provide a Hippocratic and Platonic explanation of the medical practices that he tells us come from India. He was actually referring more to the popular magical practices than to the complex Hindu medical traditions that utilized herbal medicine, as well as surgery. He accepts that he cannot understand how the *nature* of the amulets worn around the neck influences the body, but he does understand how their *properties*—through the mind—influence the bodily processes. The medical use of the placebo effect, as practiced today, is based on the premise that the substances or interventions employed are innocuous but still produce effects on the body that need to be understood, and that apparently occur through consciousness.

3   THE MAGICAL POWERS

Anthropologists have observed healing practices in many different cultures, accompanied by rituals and spells, which to some extent appear to produce beneficial effects. These practices are not always framed in elaborate explanations, as occurs in ancient medicine (Hippocratic and Vedic), but they do form part of a complex fabric of myths and rites. I am referring to shamanism, which, as performed by Qusta ibn Luqa, usually invokes a manipulation of the soul that has separated from the body of the patient; it is then necessary to elicit a process (often a journey) to recover the soul and reunite it with the body. In a certain way, the shaman proposes to manipulate the soul (or souls) to bring about its return. Significantly, shamanism, as a ritual performed by a healer or medicine man, is a widespread cultural phenomenon among the so-called primitive peoples, as they tend to be referred to, from all parts of the world; it is also an important tradition in the marginal sectors of societies isolated from scientific medicine.[1]

Qusta traveled across broad territories of the Byzantine empire; at the king's invitation, he settled in Armenia between 860 and 870, where he died at the beginning of the tenth century. No doubt he had the opportunity to observe the highly characteristic shamanic practices of the Altaic and Siberian peoples that spread to the Turks, Mongols, and Tunguses. His observations on talismans show his interest in popular magical traditions, among which shamanism stood out. The concept of shamanism arose from the study of Tungus healers, and the word *shaman,* in the language of the Tungus people, refers to the magicians and healers who predicted the future and cured the sick. The dominant idea of Altaic and Siberian shamanism is the representation of the world divided into two levels, connected by a central axis that the shaman can travel through. Shamans have the ability to enter into a trance, enabling them to go on a journey and thus cure the patient or predict the future.

Shamanism is an ancient ritual practice, as shown by the annals of the emperors of the Tang dynasty. The Turkic word *qam* is used to refer to the shaman when alluding to the magic practiced by the Kyrgyz. The compilation of these annals began in the year 941. One century after Qusta, Avicenna, the great physician and philosopher, described a Turkish shamanic ritual. In the seventeenth century, the Turkish rituals adopted the typical form ethnologists have observed in the Altai region and Siberia. The classic descriptions were extensively recorded by the Russian anthropologists V. M. Mikhailovskii (1846–1904) and S. M. Shirokogoroff (1887–1939). They meticulously depicted the activities of the shamans; their beliefs, dress, paraphernalia, and their ecstatic trances. The shaman is essentially a manipulator of spirits that sporadically enter into persons and harm them. The shaman is also invaded by the spirits but does not become possessed by them.[2] At times the shaman relates each step of the journey, in which he is searching for the soul that has escaped from the patient's body and has been abducted by bad spirits. During the trip, the shaman confronts evil powers in the form of animals that try to block his passage, but other animals help him. The shaman wears a costume that resembles an animal (a deer or bird), carries a walking stick with a horse head handle, and plays a drum decorated with drawings of the two regions of the universe and the axis that connects them. In the Ottoman era there were "babas" that traveled all over Turkey, and even when they preached the Islamic doctrine, they were actually disguised shamans that practiced the ancient magical rituals.[3] Based on the classic studies of shamanism in Siberia and the Altai region, the concept has been widely used to describe similar phenomena in other parts of the world.

An essential aspect of these rituals is the ecstatic trance entered into by the shamans. Undoubtedly, the neuronal repercussions induced by shamanic ecstasy would be interesting to study, but very little research has been conducted in that field. Nevertheless, I am more interested in exploring the relation between the shamanic ritual and the body of the patient. Do somatic effects emerge from an activity that is essentially symbolic? Are shamanic procedures efficacious in healing? In 1949 the anthropologist Claude Lévi-Strauss asked similar questions when he studied a healing chant of the Kuna Indians of Panama. By comparing the shamanic ritual with psychoanalysis, Lévi-Strauss concluded that both techniques have a "symbolic effectiveness"; in other words, an organic transformation is achieved, thanks to the fact that the patient is induced to "intensely live out a myth." The effectiveness of symbols is this "inductive property," which associates structures that are formally homologous but constructed with different materials (such as rational thought, the unconscious mind, and physiological processes),[4] signifying that an external symbolic activity causes organic changes in the body. In shamanism the patient lives out a traditional social myth, and in psychoanalysis the myth comes out of the individual history. In the former, the shaman is the one who speaks; in psychoanalysis, the analyst is silent and the patient does the talking.

A year earlier, in 1948, the Italian anthropologist Ernesto de Martino was confronted with the same problem.[5] Are the magical powers of the shamans real? From de Martino's historicist perspective, shamanic rituals are inscribed in a primitive magical world, a very different reality from our own. Thus, the shaman operates with real powers that can be proven by what de Martino calls the "scandal of research" on the capacities of clairvoyance, mind reading, telepathy, and paranormal methods of knowledge, characteristic of the Tungus shamans of Siberia. The Tungus live in a magical era, very different from the perspective of Western civilization. To illustrate his interpretation of the reality of the two worlds—the primitive magical world and the modern civilized one—de Martino also made use of the information provided by an Anglican missionary, Wilfred Barbrooke Grubb, who had worked in the Paraguayan Chaco. The example refers to a native of the Paraguayan Lengua ethnicity (the Enxet/Enlhet) who accused Grubb of having stolen some squashes from his vegetable patch, based on having seen him do so in a dream. Of course, the missionary had not stolen anything, and de Martino says that from a Western perspective it did not really happen. But strange as it may seem, he concludes that such is not the case, because the native man lives in a historical era in which what happens in dreams is included in the culturally significant reality as something experienced.[6] Grubb, in the context of the magical world, really existed in the dream of the other person, even though he had no way of knowing it.

De Martino was a disciple of the philosopher Benedetto Croce, who did not like the idea of the existence of two worlds— our Western world and the magical primitive world where paranormal, shamanic powers are real. Croce criticized the peculiar vision of "reality" of the anthropologist, who maintained that both the Lengua Indian dreamer and the missionary affirm their own particular realities.[7] Not applying the categories of historical interpretation used by ethnographers to primitive eras was unacceptable to Croce. He believed that the perpetuity of the categories, like the "unmoved mover" of which Aristotle spoke, cannot be denied.

While preparing his famous book on shamanism, the historian Mircea Eliade also published a commentary on de Martino's *Il mondo magico* (published in English as *The Primitive World*).[8] He noted that de Martino, as an idealist following Croce's teachings, was convinced that each world was a spiritual creation of man. Eliade described another of the central premises of the Italian anthropologist's book: in the primitive world, the unit of the person, his individuality, has not been developed, unlike the concept of individuality in the West. Thus, primitive peoples dramatically live under the threat of losing their self, resulting in the recurring idea we find in shamanism: the search for the lost soul. For primitive peoples, the world is never *given,* the self is never *guaranteed,* and nature is culturally conditioned; thus paranormal powers are real, even though they are not authentic in our modern Western reality. Eliade points out that de Martino remains steadfast in the purest perspective of historicist idealism: the world is not *given* to man, but rather is made by man. Eliade has a completely different interpretation; for him, paranormal phenomena are not only historically enclosed in the magical primitive world but also appear in the modern era without being an inauthentic historical regression. For Eliade, that which is sacred involves a transcendental phenomenon that can truly be experienced. According to Eliade, one must consider that there is another world, that is accessible, in principle, to *everyone* at *any time in history*. This statement connects us to the Jungian thesis of archetypes.

I wish to return to the story of the missionary and the Lengua Indian from Chaco, supposedly living in two different realities. Actually, de Martino changed the facts narrated by Grubb to adapt them to his thesis and did not tell the complete story. I suspect that he did not take the story directly from Grubb's book. In his book, the Anglican missionary explains that the Indian dreamer came from a very distant region. When Grubb explained to him that he had not been to the Indian's town for a very long time, and so could not have stolen his squashes, the Indian told him he had seen him steal three squashes in a dream. While arguing with the missionary, the Indian *clearly admitted* that the missionary had indeed *not stolen* the squashes. Nevertheless, he demanded that the missionary pay him for them because—he said—if Grubb had been there, he would have stolen them. For the Indian, what he saw in his dream was the soul of the missionary in his garden, demonstrating that he had the will or intention to steal and would have done so had the missionary's body been there. The indigenous belief was that the soul, which was perceived, thanks to the dream, could truly reveal the intention of the body. A while later, another Lengua Indian, named Puit, attempted to assassinate Grubb by shooting him with an arrow. Puit was executed by the inhabitants of his town because of *his intention,* even though he had not been successful. Grubb emphasized the huge importance of intention, more important than the acts themselves, for the Lengua people. Consequently, there was no missionary who in one world stole squashes and in the other world did not.[9]

Long before de Martino's description, the same example of the Lengua Indian from Chaco narrated by Grubb had been used by Lucien Lévy-Bruhl to describe what he called "inferior societies," characterized by their aversion to reasoning and their prelogical and mystical inclinations. I believe Lévy-Bruhl is the source of de Martino's explanation, given that he most likely did not consult Grubb's text. In his famous book from 1922, *Primitive Mentality,* Lévy-Bruhl put forward the idea that for primitive peoples, the visible world and the invisible world form a single entity.[10] To prove his thesis, he references the case of the Lengua Indian who dreamed that Grubb had stolen his squashes. He tells the complete story and understands that the problem lies in the fact that for the Indian, dreams reveal intentions, and not necessarily acts. But Lévy-Bruhl ignores the theme of intentions to instead highlight his own definition of the primitive mentality as prelogical. He supposes that the Lengua Indian accepts what the scholastics called "multipresence," that is, the simultaneous location of the same being in different places. However, such an assumption is not sustained by what Grubb narrates: the Lengua Indian did not believe that Grubb was in two places at the same time. He thought that what he had seen in his dream revealed Grubb's intentions. However, based on this supposition, Lévy-Bruhl attempts to illustrate his well-known idea that primitive people lack logic. He mistakenly assumes that the dreaming Indian is implicitly accepting something that is truly contradictory. He likens it to the belief in many "inferior" societies that the recently deceased person lying in his grave simultaneously wanders about the places where he lived. Lévy-Bruhl compares such prelogical thinking with the religious interpretation of the Eucharist, in which the body of Christ is present in different places at the same time. In said multilocation, the body continues to be one, but its presence is multiplied. Would Lévy-Bruhl have asked himself whether the belief in the multilocation of the body of Christ was a form of prelogical thinking? The problem actually did bother him, given that many years later he returned to Grubb's story in *The Notebooks on Primitive Mentality*, where he recognized that he was incorrect in having defined the Lengua Indian as possessing a prelogical mentality that fell into contradictions. Lévy-Bruhl now understood that there was no logical contradiction in the fact that it was physically impossible for Grubb to be in two places at the same time. He pointed out that Christians believe in the multipresence of God (in fact, the omnipresence of God). I must say, to be fair, in 1938, toward the end of his life, Lévy-Bruhl carried out a self-criticism of his idea of the primitive mentality in *The Notebooks:* "Let us expressly rectify what I believed correct in 1910: there is not a primitive mentality distinguishable from the other by two characteristics which are peculiar to it (mystical and prelogical). There is a mystical mentality, which is more marked and more easily observable among 'primitive peoples' than in our own societies, but it is present in every human mind."[11]

The last chapter of *Primitive Mentality* is dedicated to the relation of primitive peoples to European physicians. Lévy-Bruhl is intrigued by the fact, often related by missionaries and doctors, that upon being cured, indigenous persons, instead of being grateful, demand a payment from the European doctors for having let themselves be treated. He realizes that primitive peoples more easily accept being medicated if they trust the physician, because they presume that the medicines have mystical properties. He describes how the Gabonese Fang in Africa are surprised that the Europeans do not use any types of songs, exorcisms, or spells. In one case, the patient knew a bit of French and was not surprised by the fact that the medicine did not help him, because it was not accompanied by any ritual. The doctor that treated him had hardly spoken, and when he did it was to say "Swallow, filthy black man!" Consequently, the drug had no effect. In contrast, a doctor who always sang happy tunes while he treated his patients always had their trust. Lévy-Bruhl explains that the idea of the doctor paying the patient who lets himself be treated is based on the belief that being treated by a European causes the Indian to lose the support of the invisible forces that normally help him, making it now the responsibility of the foreigner to do so. In my opinion, this is not a convincing explanation, but strikingly, unlike Lévi-Strauss and, in a certain way, de Martino, Lévy-Bruhl showed no interest in studying whether medicine practiced with rituals could have a real and positive effect, in addition to the effect of the prescribed drugs.

My intention is not to give the impression that shamanism is a practice that only takes place in the so-called primitive societies. I have already mentioned the curative use, in modern urban societies, of magnetic necklaces and bracelets and pendants with metals that contain healing vibrations. But one of the most widespread shamanic practices in urban and industrialized societies is carried out in the many spiritualist churches found in the United States and the United Kingdom. The central axis of the ritual in these churches is the action of a medium capable of communicating with the invisible world of spirits. The medium is often a healer who contributes to alleviating afflictions, with the help of spirits. Spiritualists do not tend to use the term *shaman* to describe their mediums, but an anthropologist could easily recognize the typical practices of shamanism in such practitioners. A very revealing study was conducted by a professor at the University of Edinburgh, who himself is a medium in the spiritualist church of his town in Scotland. His fascinating book combines the objectivity of an ethnologist with the faith in his powers as a medium. During his research, he underwent step-by-step training as a medium, until achieving the ability, in sessions of meditation circles of the church, to enter into communication with the spirit-guides of dead persons who accompanied him on his journeys through the invisible world. Interestingly, this professor, David Gordon Wilson, fully accepts that it is a shamanic practice similar to those described by anthropologists, and that the medium is a shaman who possesses healing powers.[12] Lévi-Strauss would have perfectly been able to add the example of those spiritualistic congregations to his studies on the symbolic efficacy of psychoanalysis, an efficacy similar to that which occurs in shamanic practices.

4 A SHAMANIC JOURNEY IN SEARCH OF THE LOST SOUL

When Lévi-Strauss analyzed the example of the chant narrated in the ritual of a Kuna shaman (Panama), he believed he had found therein the same effective healing processes that occur in psychoanalysis. Lévi-Strauss assumed the chant was recited by the shaman during the healing ritual. That is uncertain, but the chant clearly transmitted an ancient teaching, a method of healing, in great detail. Through its examination we can follow the course of such a healing, as invoked by the shaman, at close range, with both its Kuna language version and its pictographic version available to us. The pictorial writing consists of a series of drawings in simplified form that represent the themes of the healing chant, titled *Mu-Igala* (the way of Muu); the pictures are a mnemotechnical resource for carrying out the recitation.[1] My condensed summary of the shamanic journey through the interior of the patient's body follows below.

The chant describes the afflictions of a pregnant woman who is having difficulty giving birth and details everything the shaman (*nele*) does to alleviate her condition. The woman is seated in a hammock, with her legs spread apart; the shaman is sitting under her and lights a brazier for burning cacao beans.[2] The smoke fills the hut they are in, giving powers to the healer and his helpers, who are spirits embodied in sacred images (*nuchu*). The assistants are called "plant chiefs" (*sailagan*) because of their relation to medicinal herbs, and they are preparing to face Muu, defined as the "principal grandmother," who in the Kuna cosmology is the causal force in the formation of the fetus. But Muu is also the cause of the illness afflicting the woman, who, with her legs spread apart, is bleeding and exuding fluids. The patient says that Muu wants to keep her *nigapurbalele,* her vital spirit, her soul, forever. The shaman has carved some figures out of wood (*nuchu*), which then manifest as his helpers. They, too, are now shamans (*nele,* plural *nelegan*). The *nelegan* proceed to go along the path of Muu, in the same direction the virile member uses to enter inside the woman. They walk in single file, illuminating the dark path, on a journey through the vagina to the uterus. They cross over the low mountain, the high mountain, the pointed mountain, and many more, until reaching the whirlpool (*pirya*) of Muu, where there are caimans and other horrible beasts. In the silence of midnight, the wind uproots tree trunks that block the path. The way of Muu is now an uphill path, shining in the golden hues of flames. Muu and her daughters are waiting in their house. Muu then asks, What do these shamans who are coming up along my river want? A spider that lives in the door of the house of Muu does not let them pass. There are menacing beasts at another door: a black animal shaking an iron chain, a jaguar, a red animal, a cat. Muu warns that there will be a fight with the shaman. The abode of Muu is surrounded and protected by cloth threads and curtains that turn into gold. The shaman orders the cutting of those interior threads and causes the wind to knock them down and blow them away. The path is now open. The soul (*nigapurbalele*) of the pregnant woman is there, wailing that it is Muu's prisoner and that it has been waiting for a long time. The shamans inside the blood-stained house spread smoke all around with their hats and force Muu to surrender. They take the woman's soul and her spirits and return by the same path, marching in single file, until reaching the hut where the journey began. They tell the soul: here in front of you, in the hammock, is your body, and they return it to its place. The woman is revived and the medicinal plants for completing the cure are collected. The shaman takes the plants and approaches the woman, as if he were a giant phallus, moving like the male organ, possibly to detach the placenta that has not come out and to clean and dry the interior spaces. The chant describes more rituals for preventing the woman from losing her soul again.[3] But the flow of blood has not been stopped, and more medicinal herbs are applied to control it. The midwife arrives and examines the woman's genitals and cleans them. Finally, with the help of the shaman, the infant is placed on a leaf of *urwa,* which turns red because of the blood. The chant describes how a golden river and another silver one burst in and carry away the afflictions, the caimans, the tree trunks, and finally the "golden calabash" (possibly the placenta). Gold and silver winds now blow.

It is very unlikely that a Kuna woman in the trance of a difficult delivery, suffering intense pain, could attentively follow the complicated story of the shamanic chant (which I have greatly simplified in my description). But certainly, immersed in her ethnic culture, she would have notions of the role of the shaman and the figures carved in balsam (*nuchu*), which are like an army of healers that, in procession, must penetrate the vagina to search for and capture her lost soul from the inner depths of her body. Ethnologists know that in each Kuna home there is usually a box filled with *nuchus,* each one with its personality and specific functions. Families, if they so decide, take the figurines to other houses to help cure someone who is sick. To give them power, the figurines are animated with smoke from cacao beans or pepper.[4] The anthropologist Michael Taussig believes that Lévi-Strauss imposes order on an originally disorganized and chaotic text. He does not think the chant invokes the control of chaos to give birth to a new life. He asserts that Lévi-Strauss, in his essay, actually performs a magical rite with a scientific halo. Of course, there are contradictions in the text of the chant, but it cannot be described as chaotic.[5] As I have already pointed out, what interests me is that Lévi-Strauss emphasizes the similarities between the Kuna ritual and the psychoanalytic procedure, which is why he compares the "symbolic effectiveness" of the Kuna ritual with the "symbolic realization" of the method used by the Swiss psychotherapist Marguerite Sechehaye to achieve a complete and definitive cure of a female schizophrenic patient. Sechehaye's study was published in 1947, when Lévi-Strauss was writing on the shamanism of the Kuna. Sechehaye's point of departure is her belief that the Ego of the patient has been disintegrated and that a journey is needed for its reconstruction. The Ego has supposedly suffered a regression to a magical phase, a primitive and spirit-filled stage, due to the abuse and frustration suffered by the schizophrenic woman at a very early age. Dr. Sechehaye realizes that her patient must go back (travel) to that primitive and fetal era, in which words have no meaning, resorting instead to symbols to guide the Ego on its path toward its reconstruction, like the Kuna shaman who penetrates the vagina of the woman giving birth, in search of her lost soul. To do so, the psychoanalyst could only use a language of symbolic signs, gestures, and movements to communicate with the Ego submerged in the primal magic. She utilizes symbolic objects and dolls, together with a ritual of affection. Little by little, Sechehaye says, the patient abandons her magical-animistic and artificialist behavior, to become socially adapted: the limits between the Ego and reality that had been dissolved are reestablished. There is a "symbolic realization" that reintegrates the lost Ego, a true upward march back to reality. The account of that cure is fascinating and doubtlessly evokes the shamanic ritual processes. Added to the interest aroused by the description of the method employed is the testimonial value of the diary written by the patient herself, which meticulously describes the stages of her recovery.[6]

A common denominator can be recognized in the shamanic ritual manipulations and the psychoanalytic rituals I have described: the use of symbols that are incorporated into words, objects, and actions as an expression of what physicians today call the placebo effect; the spells, necklaces, and incantations whose therapeutic properties Qusta ibn Luqa reflected upon, all carried out a function similar to the staging of the shamanic process as well as to the healing through words of the psychoanalysts. Lévi-Strauss correctly demonstrated the similarity between those healing rituals, but he did not think they could have something more in common: the placebo effect. Now I wish to directly address the study of that effect, to explore a revealing aspect of the links between the neural circuits and the phenomenon (not the epiphenomenon) of human consciousness.

5 NEUROLOGY OF THE PLACEBO EFFECT

The first thing that needs to be established is that placebos are not inert substances, but rather a set of words, rituals, symbols, and meanings that produce probable somatic effects.[1] Placebos are a kind of simulation during which pills or injections containing innocuous substances are administered or sham surgical operations are performed for the purpose of alleviating the suffering of the patient. Interest in the placebo effect began to grow at the middle of the twentieth century. One of the pioneers was the physician Henry K. Beecher, who was inspired by his experiences as a doctor during World War II in Africa and Italy and by the experiments he conducted on prisoners in Germany in the 1950s (which, rightly so, were widely criticized for ethical reasons).[2]

The placebo effect must be distinguished from other effects, such as Pavlovian conditioning. Both humans and animals can be conditioned, like Pavlov's famous dog that salivated simply with the ringing of a bell it had previously heard when given a juicy piece of meat. For example, the Pavlovian reflex has been experimented with when subjects were given a compound of

· 33

sugar pills that also contained an immunosuppressant over a period of several days. When the pill was later administered without the drug, the subjects responded as if they had taken the immunosuppressant. Something similar occurred during a taste-aversion experiment with rats. A psychologist gave them sweetened water along with an injection of a drug that induced nausea, unaware at the time of its immunosuppressive qualities. As expected, when the injections were suspended, the rats refused to drink the saccharin-flavored water. But unexpectedly, when force-fed the water, the rats gradually died from causes related to immunosuppression.[3] In another example, several subjects were injected for two consecutive days with a substance that causes an increase in hormone secretion and a decrease in cortisol levels. On the third day the patients were injected with an innocuous substance without their being aware of the change: the effects were the same as those they had initially experienced.[4] Of course, a distinction must also be made between the placebo effect and natural healing or spontaneous remission, which is not always easy to do.

The placebo effect requires the conscious participation of the patient. Dysfunction of the brain's prefrontal cortex control centers (such as occurs in Alzheimer's) halts the efficacy of the placebo. Deactivation of the frontal cortex reduces or completely suppresses the placebo effect,[5] and therefore it does not obey the same Pavlovian process of stimulus substitution. The placebo is not a sound from a bell that substitutes the stimulus of juicy meat. Harmless pills are not a mere stimulus that substitutes for a drug, like the bell of Pavlov's dog. Conditioned reflexes have been shown to be a later reaction, whereas the placebo effect is a conscious cognitive process, the result of a previous expectation. A criticism of these types of explanations is that a private subjective expectation, upon taking an innocuous pill, cannot produce a public change, visible in the physiology of the body.[6] Because of that objection, there has been a search for an alternative explanation based on "motor intentionality," as proposed by Maurice Merleau-Ponty, which describes the production of physiological effects that do not require previous concepts: the body has its environment and understands it, without the need to use symbolic functions.

Others, in the same vein as Merleau-Ponty, emphasize the importance of what they call "embodied experience," which is defined as the biological incorporation of materials arising from the social world we live in.[7] This is a way of circumventing the problem of explaining how concepts and symbols actually do produce physiological effects. Such an evasion is only necessary if a "translation" from cultural symbols to biological signals is thought to be impossible. Importantly, the proven existence of the placebo effect indicates that, somehow, such a translation does occur in humans. I will address this question further ahead.

The anthropologist Daniel Moerman suggests an amusing thought experiment for understanding the surprise doctors have felt regarding the placebo effect. Imagine we create socket wrenches that are identical to real ones in every way, except for the fact that when inserted into the socket to turn the nut, they cannot tighten it: the tool is innocuous. If we randomly place the useless socket wrenches in the toolboxes of the mechanics of a workshop, it would be very disconcerting if those instruments ended up really tightening the nuts. That is what happens when a harmless pill is randomly administered and is found to actually alleviate the patient's symptoms. This kind of thought experiment is useful for reflecting on the influence of the mechanistic model on our thinking.[8]

The placebo effect has been demonstrated in frequent clinical trials conducted by pharmaceutical laboratories to compare the efficacy of a drug with placebos. It has also been confirmed in laboratory experiments specifically designed to measure the intensity of the placebo effect. In the trials carried out by pharmaceutical companies for testing a new drug, the patients are usually advised that they can randomly receive either the placebo or the real drug. In such cases, in which the expectations of the patients are lowered, the effects tend to be minimized. Researchers must then ask the questions: Why does the placebo effect exist? Why is there an effective response when the placebo is administered during an interpersonal relation, in which the patient must be attentive and conscious? Their answer, in the form of a hypothesis, is that the placebo effect activates the self-healing functions inherent in the organism. They believe the placebo effect is efficacious for *alleviating the malaise* rather than for *curing or controlling the disease.* Consequently, they conclude, the placebo effect cannot be a result of natural selection, given that it operates mainly on the physical discomfort and not on the disease. Instead, it was a subproduct of the prolonged child-rearing period and social solidarity in the first human communities.[9]

Fabrizio Benedetti, who has studied the placebo effect for years, states that its efficacy has been clearly proven with respect to several maladies. The analgesic effect of placebos is especially noteworthy; it is the most widely studied aspect and the one that is best understood. Parkinson's disease has also been an excellent model for comprehending the organic responses to the administration of placebos. Placebo-induced immune and endocrine responses have been confirmed, as well. Seventy-five percent of the effect of drugs used to treat psychiatric disorders is believed to be attributable to the placebo effect. Likewise, the use of placebos in athletes increases their resistance and strength.[10] The relation between the placebo effect and the use of antidepressants is particularly revealing. A study on tests applied in pharmaceutical laboratories demonstrated that the placebo effect is a fundamental phenomenon: there were no significant differences between the placebo and the drug except in very severe cases of depression. In addition, the laboratory tests showed that the level of serotonin is not a determining factor in depression, given that the chemical is stimulated by certain drugs and inhibited by others, but nevertheless, similar effects are produced. If active drugs produce results that are largely a product of the placebo effect, what can be done? Because antidepressants produce strong side effects (such as sexual dysfunction, insomnia, nausea, diarrhea, and weight gain), is the prescription of placebos an option? That would involve basing treatment on a lie, which is considered ethically reprehensible.[11] Another study described the same situation: improvement of the patients was the same whether they took placebos or antidepressants, and they also improved with the so-called nonscientific "exotic therapies." Those authors emphasize that the difficulty resides in the fact that the majority of depressed patients experience spontaneous remission. But another problem is added to the ethical conflict when placebos are used: the patients end up realizing that they are not taking the effective drug because they no longer feel the side effects caused by the antidepressants.[12] Perhaps there is a false ethical problem, given that the use of placebos is a lie and a simulation that becomes true. But the massive generalization of placebos would most certainly come up against practical problems very difficult to resolve. In addition, the placebo effect serves as a shield enabling pseudoscientific treatments to flourish, such as homeopathy, which is a huge business. Thousands of persons who choose useless alternatives to cure themselves from diseases, such as cancer, die as a result of making that mistake.

The less-studied nocebo effect—the opposite of the placebo effect—is a negative consequence produced by innocuous substances. The factor that triggers the noxious effects, in contrast to the placebo, is the belief that a substance is harmful. The nocebo effect has been confirmed to cause an increase in medication-specific side effects, as was shown with finasteride in the treatment of patients with benign prostatic hyperplasia. In that study, one group of patients was given a detailed description of the possible side effects of the drug, such as erectile dysfunction, loss of libido, and ejaculation problems, and a second group was given no such information. The result was that 30.9 percent of the patients in the first group reported presenting with erectile dysfunction, whereas only 9.6 percent of the patients in the second group reported having the dysfunction. In the first group, 23.6 percent presented with decreased libido, compared with 7.7 percent in the second group. Something similar occurred with respect to ejaculation problems, but the difference was less pronounced (16.3 percent versus 5.7 percent).[13] We can suppose that the nocebo effect and the placebo effect operate through very similar processes.

The placebo effect allows us to explore a fundamental theme: the mechanisms by which cultural *symbols* are translated into neuronal *signals*. The manner by which placebos eliminate or alleviate pain has been found to be similar to that of opioid drugs such as morphine. In 1978 the analgesic effects of an inert substance were discovered to be blocked by naloxone, an opioid antagonist utilized to counteract the effects of a morphine overdose. Those analgesic effects were consequently understood to occur through the mediation of the endogenous opioid system, thanks to the activation of its μ (mu) receptors.[14] Analgesia was later confirmed to be mediated not only by the opioid system, but also through other pathways that modulate pain perception in the brain. For example, the activation of an inhibitory endorphinergic system has been studied. When the placebo produces effects in cases of lumbalgia, the endorphin level has been shown to be considerably elevated.[15] The internal pain modulation systems are influenced by emotional states and environmental eventualities. A revealing example is analgesia caused by extreme tension or stress, as in the case of athletes or soldiers who are injured in a competition or a battle and feel no pain. Incidentally, the treatment of pain is not a marginal subject. In the United States, 10 percent of the population suffers from chronic pain, and many more have pain that presents sporadically. Thus there is high opioid consumption, despite there being a malignant side effect: overdoses kill thousands of persons annually. Whether placebos could be of aid in ameliorating the crisis due to overdoses of opioids prescribed by doctors (many deaths are also caused by illegal drugs) has not been studied.

That the administration of placebos for pain activates the opioid μ receptors of the endogenous system is a fact. But as I mentioned above, analgesia is also induced in other ways and is modulated by cognitive areas of the brain, such as the language centers in the dominant hemisphere and other functional execution centers in the nondominant hemisphere. When analgesia is longer-lasting, the emotional areas located in the temporal and parahippocampal cortices tend to be involved.[16] That observation is very important, because it reveals that the effects of the placebo are tightly connected to consciousness and the emotions. Without the conscious and emotionally committed participation of the patient, the placebo effect is annulled. If the inert substances are administered when the patient is anesthetized or unconscious, they do not produce any effect. Benedetti has clearly shown that placebos activate the same biochemical pathways that are activated by drugs. Humans possess endogenous systems that can be activated by verbally induced positive expectations, by therapeutic rituals, and by different healing symbols. The placebo used as an analgesic activates at least two endogenous systems: the opioid system and the cannabinoid system. In addition, the cholecystokinergic system influences the opioid circuit, in turn stimulating different magnitudes of placebo effects. The placebo administered to patients with Parkinson's disease stimulates the release of dopamine in the striated nucleus of the brain. When morphine is injected, it binds to the opioid receptors, inhibiting the transmission of pain, but likewise, the ritual of its administration also activates those same receptors. The same thing happens when a dopaminergic drug for treating Parkinson's disease is administered: dopamine receptors are stimulated, but the ritual of its administration is also capable of stimulating them.[17]

The placebo effect is known to be more powerful when the simulation is more spectacular. Sham surgeries are much more effective than the administration of sugar pills. A study was conducted that followed two hundred patients who underwent a procedure for stent placement due to severe single-vessel stenosis. The patients were randomly allocated to undergo implantation of the device or a placebo sham procedure. The operation consisted of inserting a catheter into the artery from the groin or arm up to the point of obstruction. A balloon was then inflated to widen the vessel and introduce a metal tube, to maintain the blood flow. For the sham procedure, a catheter was actually inserted up to the blockage, but the cardiologists only pretended to perform the rest of the operation. Notably, six weeks later, no difference between the two groups operated on was detected: all the patients had less pain and passed the treadmill stress tests well.[18] So it was shown that atherosclerosis is part of a broader systemic disease whose resolution does not consist of simply unblocking arteries, as if they were clogged bathroom pipes. But what I am interested in highlighting is the fact that the more spectacular and invasive a ritual is, the greater is the placebo effect.

There are numerous and varied examples of how the placebo influences the course of illnesses.[19] The cases I have summarized help us understand that we are dealing with a process of translation of the meanings and symbols involved in the healing ritual into neurochemical signals in the endogenous systems of the central nervous system. The words and paraphernalia that doctors use are translated into flows of endorphins, opioids, dopamine, and serotonin that influence the functioning of the brain and the biological processes of the organism. I believe the placebo effect reveals the presence of a system of symbolic substitution of elements missing in the biological process. The biological process of healing or alleviation is completed (or is better completed) with the support of symbolic prostheses. The prostheses are formed by the healing rituals that, like the test of the placebo effect, importantly influence the course of a malady, even in the absence of the support of active drugs. This can only occur through the translation of cultural symbols into neurochemical signals. How that translation of symbols into chemical codes takes place needs to be studied with precision.

It is a feedback mechanism, due to the fact that the positive results of the placebo effect stimulate the extension and consolidation of the healing rituals. But another neuronal dimension must be added to the endogenous processes stimulated by the placebos. The feedback is a circuit that passes through a person's emotional system. As has been seen, the healing effect of the placebo only occurs through the cognitive system: if conscious mechanisms do not function, there is no relief. The process is mediated by consciousness. But there is also no placebo effect, without an emotional response of well-being or calm. And emotions, as Antonio Damasio has explained so well, are complicated series of chemical and neural responses that involve the secretion of hormones (such as cortisol), peptides (such as the β endorphin), monoamines, norepinephrine, serotonin, and dopamine.[20]

We are dealing with a circuit that begins with the words of the physician, a type of shaman in a white coat, that stimulate neurochemical mechanisms of alleviation. In turn, those mechanisms of relief produce emotional states of well-being, pleasure, and calm that additionally stimulate expressions and feelings of confidence toward the physician. Physicians are supported by that confidence when they perform their healing rituals. The circuit is understood to pass through the conscious symbolic organizing principles as well as through the neurochemical systems of the brain. A tight network of interconnections connects the biological spaces with the cultural ones.

6 ON ELECTRONIC AMULETS AND CATHARSIS

Medical rituals are part of an ensemble of instruments, machines, objects, and symbols that converge around us, providing us with support, relief, and information while also communicating with us, entertaining us, and helping us in our work. A good part of these ceremonial and symbolic prostheses that swirl about our surroundings every day contribute to producing calm, well-being, and pleasure. They are largely an extension of consciousness. They also amuse us and make us think. They create an agreeable, tranquil, and even entertaining environment, but with fractures that cause malaise, tension, disgust, anger, fear, or sadness. An extraordinary example of such a cultural and symbolic prosthesis connecting us with the environment is the smartphone. Its enormously extensive use has turned it into a very important part of the exocerebrum. In addition to its primary function of enabling us to have long-distance communication with others, it allows us to navigate the internet, send and receive all kinds of messages through WhatsApp, Skype, Twitter (X), or Facebook, listen to music, read newspapers and books, consult maps to guide us, direct us through city traffic, purchase items in the blink of an eye, request an Uber, rent an Airbnb, and much more. It is a small electronic exocerebrum that connects our central nervous system with a broad social and cultural universe. The smartphone has come to play a significant role in the potential well-being of millions of people, even though it also channels tensions and distress. The device is also a kind of intelligent robot that, while forming part of our consciousness, is not conscious itself.

The smartphone could be said to be a hyperdeveloped version of the amulets and necklaces referred to by Qusta ibn Luqa, the physician I spoke of at the beginning of these reflections. The smartphone concentrates a huge quantity of symbolic functions and produces a placebo effect similar to the effect produced, according to Qusta, by charms and incantations. The smartphone is a portable amulet, like those that generated healing effects in ancient times, and is endowed with immense symbolic power. Most certainly, when a patient of Qusta's lost the amulet hanging from his or her neck, it was a great source of anxiety for that person, akin to the so-called *nomophobia*, a term coined in a 2010 study commissioned by the UK Post Office that analyzed the tensions produced by smartphone separation or loss on the users of said prosthesis. The term is an abbreviated form of the phrase "no mobile phone phobia" and refers to the fear of not being in contact with the environment because of losing or being separated from the mobile device. Of course, the smartphone is much more than an amulet considered to have beneficial powers. Moreover, the harmful effects produced by the lack of contact with the electronic prosthesis go far beyond the so-called nocebo effect, which, as I have previously stated, is the opposite of the placebo effect: the nocebo effect derives from the belief that medications or medical interventions produce deleterious results, even though innocuous substances have been employed or sham surgeries performed. It is also similar to the harm arising from the belief that a witch can cast the evil eye on someone. Indeed, both beneficial and harmful effects can result from the manipulation of the symbolic systems people are connected to.[1]

We are now coming up against the problem of the effects of subjective sensations on the functioning of consciousness. Years ago, a specialist in consumerism observed that the possessions of individuals were seen as part of their identity. Russell Belk, expanding on the concept of William James, stated that humans are what they possess.[2] In fact, he referred mainly to the subjective sensation of the extension of the ego and was not concerned with investigating whether the possessions of an individual could *really* be an extension of consciousness, as I believe is the case. In the same line of thought, recent studies on the impacts of communication media have proposed that, just as there is an iPhone, there is also an iSelf and an iEgo. The particle i, used by the famous brand of smartphones, is utilized to denote the extension of consciousness through electronic means. The physiological and psychological influence of the lack of access to the smartphone (nomophobia) was analyzed in a study. When separated from their mobile devices, the participants' cognitive test grades were lower, their level of anxiety increased, their heart rate was higher, and their blood pressure rose. When the individuals in the experiment got their phones back, their cognitive scores improved and their heart rate and blood pressure normalized. The conclusion was that the study participants considered the telephonic device to be an amplification of self, and this extension of consciousness improved their situation. The deprivation of their smartphones caused the participants to have poorer results on the cognitive tests and greater physiological anxiety.[3] Given that the smartphone is a robot that extends the powers of our ego, the examination of different kinds of robots is the theme of the second part of this book, in which I explore whether such machines could be capable, on their own, of developing an artificial form of consciousness.

It is well known that the neural mechanisms of pleasure are more poorly understood than the processes of pain. The analgesic and alleviation effects that placebos produce are widely studied, whereas there is little interest in analyzing their hedonic effects. Researchers interested in the latter found that alleviation effects are only half the story. The other half are effects of enhanced pleasure, or hyperhedonia.[4] They have found that the effects of analgesia and the effects of pleasure activate the same circuits in the brain. They conclude in their study that pleasure and pain display similarities in neurochemical and neurophysiological terms, comparing the cerebral processes of hyperhedonia and analgesia, with respect to the placebo effect. The results showed that the expectation of enhanced pleasure (placebo hyperhedonia) increased sensory activation, whereas the expectation of pain relief (placebo analgesia) decreased sensory activation. Hyperhedonia and analgesia appear to share the same mechanisms. I mentioned before that analgesic effects are mediated by the opioid system, as well as by the neural pathways that modulate pain in the central nervous system.

The rituals of pleasure lead us to the ancient idea of catharsis, a notion that the Greeks associated with the grand spectacle of the theater. The metaphor of catharsis has its origin in Hippocratic medicine, which recommended the elimination of the bad bodily humors for healing the patient and reestablishing balance in the body. The bleeding and purging used by the ancient physicians to restore corporeal equilibrium were not pleasurable healing methods, but nevertheless, relief was expected to follow the treatment. In contrast, Aristotle took the idea of catharsis and associated it with the pleasure produced by the tragedies performed in the theater. In his *Poetics,* catharsis has an important metaphorical connotation: it is a theatrical representation that produces emotions that purify the audience through a pleasure that shocks. The tragedy releases them from the same fears and horrors it represents. It is a tragic pleasure that purifies and heals the spectators, ridding them of their afflictions and distress. In his *Politics,* Aristotle refers to the cathartic effects of music. Music sometimes produces a religious frenzy in its listeners, healing those participating in the orgiastic ritual. At other times, music is simply an innocent and gentle pleasure that relaxes people.

The concept of catharsis was used by the physician Josef Breuer to refer to a healing practice that consisted of letting neurotic patients speak freely, while under hypnosis, so they could release their emotions. That method was taken up again by Freud, who then developed the treatment, eliminating the hypnosis. And so, psychoanalysis was born. Freud recognized it was actually an ancient method that stimulated psychic states in the patient that were favorable to healing. He pointed out that primitive peoples used psychotherapy, almost exclusively, for curing the sick. Freud said that potions, magic formulas, purifying ablutions, or the provocation of prophetic dreams were therapeutic because they were accompanied by a psychic treatment: the magic of the word, which could eliminate morbid manifestations, especially those based on emotional states. Hence began what Freud called the "treatment of the soul"

(*Seelenbehandlung*).⁵ This therapeutic action was based on the use of words, through suggestion, and its origin was Breuer's technique of "hypnotic suggestion." Recalling the old saying that neuroses are not cured by medicine but by the physician, whose personality exerts a strong psychic influx, Freud alludes to hypnotic suggestion and to therapies that use distraction and entertainment. However, he says he is inclined toward the method that Breuer called *cathartic,* and which he prefers to call *analytic.*⁶ Freud did not use the concept of the placebo to refer to the magic of the word or to catharsis. Many persons today believe that psychoanalysis is actually a manifestation of the placebo effect. But in the analytic treatment it is the patient, not the physician, who does most of the speaking. Nevertheless, the doctor conducts the ritual in a space, the consultation office, that is specially prepared for stimulating catharsis. Importantly, the patient firmly believes in the virtues and efficacy of the cathartic process directed by the analyst, even though it is difficult and painful.

Psychoanalysis is based on the somewhat unlikely idea that the therapeutic ritual enables the unconscious to flow into the sphere of the conscious. According to Freud, the emergence of the unconscious is linked to sensations of unpleasure, and as a result, is rejected. Thus, the physician must guide the patient to accept something that until then had been rejected (repressed) due to the automatic regulation determined by unpleasure.⁷ The unpleasure that psychoanalytic catharsis causes appears to be more similar to the unpleasant Hippocratic purges than to the tragic Aristotelian pleasure. It is possible that what actually occurs during the psychoanalytic ritual is a flow of the conscious into the sphere of the unconscious, because the almost magical conviction that the treatment is beneficial is precisely what stimulates the neurochemical (obviously not conscious) processes that produce the patient's well-being.

In the example of the successful treatment of a schizophrenic patient carried out by the Swiss psychoanalyst Marguerite Sechehaye, which I mentioned in a previous chapter, a notable modification in the method must be specified. The cathartic analysis directed at making the patient speak only resulted in temporary relief, and so the treatment had to be changed, utilizing a new technique: one eliciting the symbolic realization of the unconscious desires of the schizophrenic girl. The active spoken, ritualistic, and symbolic intervention of the psychoanalyst was needed for the patient to be cured.

The placebo effect must operate on the basis of the conscious, not the unconscious. In this sense, although we have every indication that the placebo effect is at work in psychoanalysis, the theoretical presuppositions of psychotherapy go in a very different direction. They are, in fact, based on the postulation that during the treatment a verbal flow emerges from repressed memories stored within the mysterious realm of the unconscious mind. My interest here is not to critique Freudian theories but rather to show how the placebo effect provides proof that the symbolic structures lodged in the social and cultural networks not only influence the functioning of the brain but are also a constitutive part of human consciousness, a consciousness mounted in both the neuronal tissue and the symbolic textures that surround us. Reflecting upon the widespread rituals of pleasure and the word is a way to confront and explain the mystery of human consciousness.

7   ZOMBIES AND TRANSHUMANISTS

Those who try to understand the phenomenon of consciousness attach great importance to feelings, whether they manifest as pleasure, pain, or in many other ways. A strongly emphasized notion is that the essential question of the relation between the mind and body can be better understood as a relation between sensations and functions. Hence, a very basic question for many philosophers arises—one that has yet to be answered: Why do we not just carry out functions, instead of having sensations? Instead of being felt, why is pain or pleasure not merely "functioned"? Why are we not like zombies, those unfeeling beings invented by philosophers that only perceive signals that activate functional responses? Those questions will most certainly have to be answered if the mystery of consciousness is to be deciphered. We must know how and why we have sensations and not simply prove that there are correlations between a given conduct and certain sensations.[1] For example, when we translate a sensation of pain to communicate it through speech, thereby letting others know we are confident they can also experience the same unpleasant sensation, many believe we are not understanding the how and the why of consciousness, because our symbolic description of pain could work just as well, even if our complaints did not correspond to a given sensation. We only know that we feel pain because we experience it, but we do not know why we feel it. We do not know why a function of the brain should be felt, instead of just being "functioned."

The zombie argument, which is very popular among philosophers of the English-speaking world, has been utilized to support the idea of the existence of beings (or machines) just like us, except for the fact that they would not possess consciousness. Such zombie-like beings would be theoretically identical to humans, both in their behavior and their functioning, but would not have experiences. There are those who conclude that the logical possibility of an unfeeling and unconscious zombie would demonstrate the actual presence of a metaphysical substance in humans, such as the soul, that animates consciousness and creates sensations. The thought experiment of the zombie attempts to demonstrate the possibility that consciousness and the functioning of the body have a logical and separate existence.

The fascination with the zombie appears to compel us to ask a question aimed at God. Why are we not zombies? Why must we suffer? We can find the answer in the Bible: suffering is the consequence of original sin. Thinkers obsessed with the zombie theory have not realized that, in the Bible, we can find an ancient example of beings identical to humans but lacking feelings and consciousness. I am referring to Adam and Eve before they ate the fruit from the tree of knowledge in the Garden of Eden. In my slightly playful interpretation, before eating the forbidden fruit, Adam and Eve were immortal beings, lacking a consciousness that would allow them to distinguish between good and evil. They were naked like the animals, with no feelings of shame. Perhaps Eve, prodded by the serpent, was not quite as insensitive, given that she was curious and wanted to taste the forbidden fruit. But I like to imagine that the two inhabitants of Paradise were zombies, free from pleasures and woes, before their fall into sin. In that line of interpretation, Saint Augustine was well aware that if Adam had not sinned, he would have been able to perform a function, such as the erection of the penis, with neither libido nor passion, using his erect organ in the same way man plants seeds in the earth with his hand, to penetrate an equally unfeeling and frigid Eve, who was functionally capable of procreating without pain.[2] Why did humans not remain original zombies, like Adam and Eve? The religious response is obvious: because of the sin that brought unknown emotions, pain, suffering, consciousness, and other sensations, we can suppose, such as pleasure and joy.

And so, the zombie argument could have a religious undertone. Seen in that light, the mystery of consciousness would appear not to have a scientific solution. But if we consider the idea that consciousness extends outside of the brain, we can probably come closer to an explanation. Nevertheless, there has been significant resistance to such an idea: Why would I want to look for extensions of my headache in a place outside of the cranium? It would appear that my ability to name and explain my pain has nothing to do with the subjective sensation. But we humans use words to refer to suffering and possible cures. The issue is not that others only know of my pain because I explain it. The use of speech is an essential element of consciousness. An animal lacking language cannot *know* that it feels a given pain:

it experiences the pain but is not conscious of doing so. Obviously, many other animals besides humans suffer, but they do not know that they feel pain. Suffering that is accompanied by words and pain that is caused only by signals are two very different things. Confusion arises from the fact that for neuroscientists, such as Stevan Harnad, consciousness is the same as feeling, whereas I suggest that the use of words, and more broadly a complex symbolic system, is added to sensations. Other neuroscientists, such as Gerald Edelman, understand that the zombie argument is a logical impossibility and that the neural process forming the biological base of consciousness cannot function without the simultaneous existence of consciousness.[3] Therefore, demanding an answer as to how and why we are not as insensitive as zombies is a way of invoking an unsolvable mystery.

Without a doubt, human consciousness is based on the feelings a living being possesses. But there is a peculiar sensitivity that must be understood, which in turn can explain the subjective sensations. When the cerebral circuits connect to the symbolic networks of the cultural environment, they simultaneously perceive the unfamiliar and external nature of the forms of linguistic, visual, musical, and instrumental communication that are characteristics of society. That sensitivity, based on neuronal incompleteness, together with the recognition of the strangeness of the symbols that connect us with other humans, is the reason the individual ego, unique and conscious, comes into being.

The placebo effect is an example of how sensitivity and the use of words are interlinked. Speech, as I have shown, is a powerful prosthesis that, in the context of medical or shamanic rituals, can alleviate some types of suffering and provide pleasures and satisfactions. The idea that ritual and symbolic prostheses can create extraordinary biological effects and contribute to healing has extended to what could be called, if we wish to see it with a bit of irony, a postmodern shamanism: transhumanism. Therein, rituals and simulations are substituted by prostheses actually implanted in the body of humans to enhance their capacities. Words are substituted by artifacts. An attempt is made to hybridize that which is human with the machine, to stimulate cognitive and biological progress through the creation of a new posthuman species: cyborgs. Physicians will then be able to directly treat physical diseases and mental disorders by means of a brain that is improved and enhanced by technology. The leading promoter of transhumanism, Ray Kurzweil, is convinced that humans can become much more intelligent and much healthier through intracerebral implants.[4] Such a claim implicitly recognizes the close relation between the brain and the exocerebrum, but the transhumanists want to go a step further and incorporate the exocerebral mechanisms into the same body containing the brain, through hypersophisticated technological implants. But in transhumanism, the relation between the brain and the symbolic environment becomes a tight link that attaches the human body to program-operated cybernetic and robotic artifacts. According to Kurzweil, a future human condition, in which thousands of nanorobots circulate through our blood and in our brain to fight against pathogens, correct errors in DNA, eliminate toxins, and perform tasks that will improve our physical well-being, is not far off. There will be an interaction between nanorobots and neurons, with the latter being replaced by longer lasting and more efficient nonbiological versions.

The transhumanists tend to think that the arrival of a technological singularity in the not-too-distant future will result in the production of posthuman beings. They believe we will be seeing those formidable mutations in just a few decades, through their trust in the exponential acceleration of the biocybernetic technologies. I think they are mistaken as to the imminent arrival of the mutations. At present the transhumanists seem rather like shamans who travel to the future and predict the situation of organs replaced by technologically sophisticated prostheses, to arrive at a utopian condition. There is a religious ingredient in the hope of the coming of the Singularity, with an uppercase *S*, that will open the door to a new age.

A lower-case singularity is the one that makes us human, that of artificial prostheses that constitute culture and the social environment we humans have created. It is the singularity that brings speech and sensitivity together, into a single network. The new Singularity of the transhumanists appears to be the transformation of portions of our artificial exocerebrum into a new internal, mechanical artificiality, implanted for the purpose of "improving" and "enhancing" human abilities. In its extreme form, that transformation would be a synthetic reduction of parts of the symbolic cultural and social space that surrounds us into a set of *internal* cybernetic devices. The "enhanced human" of transhumanism would be endowed with a continuation of the artificial nature of the exocerebrum, through cybernetic and electromechanical means. The primitive amulets and spells, together with the medical rituals that increase the curative potentialities of drugs and surgeries, would be the embryo that gives way to the new humans of the future, who, thanks to the magic of technology, will interiorize the properties of the exocerebrum, marginalize the biological body, and eliminate the forms of individual consciousness we presently know. They would possibly be new zombies, dispossessed of the bothersome sensitivity imposed upon us by our biological bodies. For that posthuman condition to arrive, a form of artificial consciousness must emerge, a problem I will address in the second part of this book.

Part II
THE CONSTRUCTION OF AN ARTIFICIAL CONSCIOUSNESS
ANTHROPOLOGY OF THE ROBOTIC EFFECT

8 THE MYSTERY OF THINKING MACHINES

The exocerebral circuits of human consciousness are completely artificial. They have no organic nature. They form part of culture and the extensive social networks that surround us. But they are capable of affecting how neural circuits function, as I have shown in my reflections on the influence placebos have on the brain. The artifacts of both medical and shamanic rituals, as well as their simulations, produce effects on the neuronal biochemistry. Some segments of the exocerebral circuits are mechanical prostheses that possess artificial intelligence, such as computers or smartphones. When intelligent digital and electronic prostheses connect to the brain, they are transformed into an artificial or inorganic part of our consciousness. Obviously, the study of how these artificial segments of consciousness behave is of great importance in understanding the potential expansion of machines endowed with a powerful artificial intelligence capable of reaching human and even superhuman levels, and begs the question: Could machines equipped with such advanced intelligence someday develop characteristics similar to human consciousness and autonomy? I will take an imaginary flight into the future to explore the possible answers to that query.

To do so, my necessary point of departure is a theory of consciousness. There are those who, like Susan Blackmore, believe that consciousness is an illusion, a phenomenon that exists but is not what it seems.[1] She arrives at the conclusion that any machine capable of imitation could acquire this type of illusion. Blackmore says it is an illusion created by memes for the purpose of reproducing themselves, but in reality it is nothing other than the false idea of a conscious ego that persists throughout a lifetime. She has adopted the theory of memes, proposed by Richard Dawkins, who conceived the idea of the existence of cultural information conglomerates that function like biological genes.

The theory of memes is the basis for believing that robots designed to imitate humans could acquire the illusion of an ego and a consciousness in the same way humans do. The machines capable of imitating and copying could house an evolutionary process of their memes that would lead them to eventually becoming self-replicating entities, without the process of emergence being controlled by humans. Such robots would spontaneously invent these processes of self-replication. They would be machines that, like us, possess the peculiar illusion of being conscious. An illusion is something that deceives or that causes a false interpretation. The reasons why Blackmore thinks she knows that consciousness is a false interpretation, an illusion, are unclear. When she put forward her idea to the philosopher John Searle, he rejected it, saying that if someone has the illusion of being conscious, then that person is conscious. The distinction between appearance and reality cannot be applied to consciousness.[2] That the memes operating in robots could create the same false impression of housing an ego endowed with continuity is deduced from the definition of human consciousness as an illusion. If our consciousness is an illusion, then we have to try to explain why we are conscious of the fact that our consciousness is an illusion, forcing us to enter into a useless infinite regression, as explained by the philosopher Peter Farleigh.[3]

The problem with Blackmore's theory is that it is based on the working of supposed basic units of information—memes—whose existence has never been proven and whose definition is conspicuous by its absence. But since artificial intelligence and robots function through copying, replication, and information computation processes, it seems easy to suppose that someday consciousness will appear in machines capable of imitating and copying, the same way in which memes supposedly sparked human consciousness. From that perspective, it is a question of waiting until the builders of artificial intelligence systems, supported by the extraordinary speed at which technology develops, are able to create robots that are so powerful they can evolve into human-like forms of consciousness. It is a legitimate hope that leads us to speculate whether it will take decades, centuries, or millennia for that extraordinary singularity to emerge.

At the opposite pole, we have the opinion of the mathematician Roger Penrose, who is convinced that consciousness is based on noncomputational processes. Consequently, for Penrose, it is impossible for an artificial intelligence system to develop a conscious mind like that of a human. He is certain that a conscious mind cannot be produced by an algorithm, through a computer.[4] Searle also believes that digital machines, with their algorithms, are incapable of understanding what they do. Even though he accepts the idea that the brain functions like a computer algorithm, he believes that consciousness can only emerge if the program incarnates in a biological body and not in a machine. However, Searle's reasoning for why he thinks organic hardware is an inevitable necessity for housing the software inscribed in the central nervous system is not clear.

In my opinion, these discussions show that the exploration of the theoretical territory of consciousness and artificial intelligence systems is a good opportunity for scrutinizing the various theories that try to explain the way in which the human mind creates a personal identity and draws the outline of that self. For their part, the engineers dedicated to building and programming intelligent machines need theoretical guidelines for orienting them in their work if they intend to create artificial consciousnesses. Admittedly, the construction of intelligent and conscious machines does not have to exclusively follow the human model. But undoubtedly the example of human consciousness embodied in a biological organism can stimulate the new engineers of souls.

From my point of view, consciousness is not only a biological phenomenon. Consciousness is a hybrid phenomenon that connects neural circuits with sociocultural networks. It is a convergence of apparently electrochemical signals in the brain with cultural symbols in the social environment. That congregation is particularly important in the instances when humans realize, not without anxiety, they cannot have blind faith in their biological resources to survive or overcome difficulties. They have to resort to extrasomatic supports provided by culture. Under such circumstances, the cerebral circuits connect to cultural prostheses. And when such a connection is made, the sparks of consciousness (of the self) jump, given that the neural networks perceive the exteriority and foreignness of those symbolic and linguistic channels. The neural circuits are sensitive to their incomplete nature. I like to think they have the sensitivity of the hermit crab, which, when it grows, has to leave an empty exoskeleton behind to be able to live in a larger one. Human consciousness has that kind of sensitivity when facing the incompleteness of the cerebral circuits; at the same time, it reacts to the fact that the cultural prostheses it connects to are unfamiliar and nonbiological. The result is the distinctive subjectivity that characterizes humans and is so hard to explain. The cerebral conditions responsible for this singular sensitivity continue to be a mystery that neuroscientists have to clarify. They are the springs of a connection between biological signals and cultural symbols, two very different spheres that interact in a very precise and astounding manner. A unified theory that encompasses the two spheres has not yet been postulated, in the same way that physicists have not been able to unify quantum mechanics with gravity.

The theme of robot sensitivity reminds me of an 1810 essay by the great writer Heinrich von Kleist, which for me is a literary key for entering into the subject of artificial consciousness. The German dramatist was obsessed with the conflict between the emotions and reason. When he studied mathematics and read Kant, he lost faith in knowledge and believed that the separation between the ego and its environment revealed a tragic division between the subject and knowability: hence, humans were condemned to uncertainty.

In *Über das Marionettentheater,* an essay in the form of a dialogue, Kleist tells the story of a very popular dancer, his friend, who often went to see the presentations of a very successful marionette theater in the market square. The puppets moved with such extraordinary grace that the dancer felt they surpassed humans. The puppeteer would be like the programmer of a robot, who skillfully produces the movement of an inanimate object. Kleist tells his friend that the puppeteer can make the marionettes dance with no input of his own feelings or sensations, like an organ grinder turning the handle of his instrument. The dancer replies that such is not the case, because the puppeteer's fingers are related to the marionettes, like the relation of numbers to algorithms or asymptotes to hyperbolas. But he did believe that the traces of human will could be removed from the puppets, so that their dancing was exclusively created by mechanical forces. Something like that happens with the engineer who programs a robot: he projects his feelings into algorithms that animate the totally unconscious movements of the machine.

The dancer believes that if an artisan creates a marionette, according to the instructions he has imagined, the puppet could dance much better than the greatest human dancers. And, as if he had foreseen the sophisticated robotic prostheses we are familiar with today, he gave the example of artificial legs made by English artisans to replace the limbs lost by unfortunate persons. The dancer maintains that the individuals using them are able to dance with surprising elegance, reminding me of the model Aimee Mullins, whose legs were amputated when she was a child and who became famous for her athletic achievements with the aid of various types of sophisticated prostheses. The marionettes that the dancer has designed in his head would execute their steps with a high level of flexibility, lightness, and harmony. But the great advantage of the puppets is that they can act without being affected; they are lifeless because the puppeteer controls them with his strings, and so they move like simple pendulums, governed only by the law of gravity, which is an excellent quality the majority of human dancers do not have. In addition, these marionettes have the advantage of being almost as light as air, and so are free from the greatest obstacle in dance: body weight. Likewise, the engineer who builds a robot knows the machine is not alive and is free from the weight of the troubles that affect human beings.

Dancers are too conscious of each one of their movements. Kleist tells his friend that he will never believe that a mechanical puppet can be as graceful as a living human body. The dancer responds that, with respect to grace and elegance, a human will never be able to reach the level of a marionette. He finds the explanation in the third chapter of the book of Genesis: consciousness hinders natural grace, that innocence present in the original Paradise before Adam and Eve ate the fruit of the tree of science. It must be understood that the spirit cannot err where there is no spirit, as with marionettes. Thus, continuing with the parallelism, unconscious zombies, artificial androids, could act better and be more intelligent than the humans who have created them. In the organic world, says the dancer, to the degree that reflection dims and weakens, grace emerges with more decision and brilliance. Grace flows with great purity where there is no consciousness or where consciousness is infinite. In other words, it appears in a marionette or in a god. Kleist, astonished, asks him if we should eat from the tree of knowledge again, to return to the original state of innocence. The dancer tells him, yes, but that it will be the last chapter in the history of the world. One year after writing that essay, Kleist came to the final chapter in the history of his life, after sealing one of the most famous suicide pacts in the history of literature. His beloved friend Henriette Vogel was terminally ill and apparently asked him to kill her. They went to the shore of the Kleiner Wannsee, a lake outside of Berlin; there, Kleist shot her dead and killed himself immediately afterward.

Did Kleist commit suicide because he realized that he could never be like the marionettes or the gods? Perhaps he could not bear the weight of his solitary and limited consciousness. That is why the puppeteer he described in his essay made sure to extinguish the sparks of consciousness that could switch on the inanimate doll. In contrast to those of a puppet, the sparks of consciousness in humans jump when their neural circuits connect with exocerebral prostheses. Even though Kleist's reflections are over two centuries old, if we apply them to the relation between humans and robots they acquire a current relevance, leading us to the ethical question: Is the human desire to build machines endowed with an artificial consciousness a reckless impulse? Is it not better to leave machines without consciousness, like Kleist's marionettes? He would watch, with alarm, the possibility of transmitting the sin of consciousness to intelligent machines, and would most certainly prefer that they remain unfeeling robots.

9   THE ROBOTIC EFFECT

When a physician or a shaman performs a symbolic ritual, it usually produces a demonstrable biological effect, the so-called placebo effect. Similarly, when an engineer creates a program and inserts it into a machine, it produces a useful mechanical effect, which could be called the robotic effect. In both cases there is an intellectual artifact that produces tangible effects on a body, whether organic or mechanical. The placebo effect involves an indispensable requirement, one it cannot work without: the subject whose body is to be healed must be *fully conscious* of the fact that he or she is undergoing a healing process. But the person in question is *not conscious* of being given an innocuous drug. Conversely, the machine endowed with a computer program *is not conscious* of what is happening, which does not prevent the robotic effect from being produced, and the device goes to work, directed toward a predetermined goal. The scientific community does not believe that robots, as we know them today, have a consciousness similar to that of humans (or even to that of a mouse or rabbit).

The robots we know at present are machines that can perform tasks relatively autonomously, perceive their surroundings, and act intentionally, because an artificial intelligence created by a human engineer is incorporated in them.[1] It is not common for robots to autonomously be capable of obtaining the energy needed for their sustenance. They do not repair themselves, they do not physically grow, nor do they reproduce, making copies of themselves. Having the ability to achieve such feats is not impossible, and in fact attempts have already been made to overcome those inadequacies. For example, a robot called EcoBot III has an artificial digestive system that functions with a microbial fuel cell capable of producing electrical energy from a biochemical reaction. This artificial digestive system feeds on flies. In its first version, the EcoBot, capable of moving by means of self-generated electrical energy, had to be fed manually. In its latest version, the apparatus possesses a sophisticated system that attracts the flies through colors and smells. The trapped flies fall into a deposit containing a bacterial soup that digests and degrades the insects to produce the electricity necessary for feeding the robot's motor. The EcoBot moves about on wheels in a puddle of water, in a closed tank full of flies. It takes in the water that its metabolism requires through a tube. This experimental model is the only existent robot capable of autonomously obtaining the food it needs for producing enough energy to move and work.[2]

The physical self-repair of a robotic system is something that presently exists only in the imagination. Robots do not heal themselves, nor do they repair one of their components if it breaks down. They do not physically grow over time. Nevertheless, at the purely computational level it is possible to create growth and self-repair programs without being connected to operating machines. Reproduction through data copying and replication is also possible at this level. There are very sophisticated and complex computational models capable of imitating very diverse biological, neuronal, and social processes.

An example that is more than a model or a simulation, because it has a practical and precise use, is the so-called Intelligent Distribution Agent (IDA), developed for the United States Navy.[3] After completing a series of tasks, sailors must be assigned a new set of duties. The IDA system, which completely automates the distribution and assignment of duties, is used for that purpose. IDA does so through email communications with the sailors, engaging in normal conversations with them, producing letters that appear to be written by humans. As an agent, IDA must adapt to the needs of the Navy, the established rules, the estimated costs, and the desires and needs of each individual sailor. IDA is capable of processing the messages it receives, in natural language. In its own way, it understands, recognizes, and classifies the content of the messages. Although its "comprehension" is very elemental and superficial, it is sufficient for processing information. IDA has memories and a workspace, where it processes the information it receives. It is even capable of simulating emotions, such as showing anxiety, when it does not convince a sailor to accept a task, or frustration, when it does not understand a message. The system operates with many relatively independent, special-purpose miniprocesses (called *codelets*), which enable IDA to create possible scenarios and plans of action, to then later choose the most adequate. IDA can thus offer sailors options regarding a task and is capable of negotiating changes to satisfy the service members. With the work IDA carries out, it learns through associative processes.

IDA's creator, Stan Franklin, does not ascribe a phenomenal consciousness to his artifact; rather, he believes attributing this type of consciousness to machines simply involves an attitude on the part of those who observe the artifact. It is merely a question of the attribution of consciousness, and so he predicts that someday sufficiently intelligent, capable, and communicative agents will be programmed, and as a result, humans will only assume they are conscious artifacts. From such a perspective, the question of machine consciousness will no longer be relevant.[4]

Another expert in robotics, Alan Winfield, has come to similar conclusions. He is convinced that, in principle, it will be possible in the future to build an android as perfect as Data, the famous robot from the series *Star Trek: The Next Generation*. Such humanoid robots could be designed to behave as if they were conscious, so convincingly, that they could not be thought of otherwise. But Winfield adds an ironic note: such perfect imitations would also be capable of arguing with a philosopher and convincing the thinker that he or she is not really conscious, but merely a robot. Such a machine would gain our trust, our respect, and a recognition of its own identity, challenging our deeply rooted ideas about what it means to be human.[5] From the perspective of robotic engineering, there is no need to wait for philosophers or neuroscientists to resolve the mystery of consciousness. In fact, engineers may end up contributing to solving the mystery by building increasingly more capable and intelligent robots.

From a technological perspective, the construction of robots does not require a precise terminology. Vincenzo Tagliasco has written that, unlike scientific work (which requires definitions), technology overcomes ambiguities when the designs are brought to life, through the construction of prototypes that have to function correctly in the real world. To build a machine with a "minimal consciousness," the experiences of the artifact must push it to seek out new experiences, maintain a record of them, unify the information, and be capable of defining new motivations that have the same predefined objectives that were designed and materially inscribed in the apparatus. Tagliasco concludes that artificial consciousness will not result from a scientific discipline but rather will emerge as a consequence of a technological endeavor that is closer to robotics than to neuroscience or psychology.[6]

The goal, from that perspective, is to build an apparently conscious robot that behaves as such. Robotics can put aside emotions, pleasures, feelings, pain, and desires and can forget about blood, flesh, and hormones to concentrate on building increasingly sophisticated machines that someday, it is hoped, will create an extraordinary technological singularity: the emergence of artificial intelligence systems much more powerful than the intellect nature has bestowed upon humans.[7] The robotic effect is produced when a machine controlled by a program is transformed into an artifact that demonstrates an intelligence and behavior that appears to be human. In its most advanced version—imagined, desired, and feared, but still very far off—it will display all the symptoms of possessing a consciousness very similar to ours, blurring the lines of certainty that the robot is, in fact, nothing more than a very efficient zombie. In the robotic effect, the human engineer builds complex and intelligent prostheses that are part of the consciousness of their creators. Engineers dream of a future when machines will achieve an autonomy that would free the prostheses from their owners and creators. By acquiring forms of autonomous consciousness, the enslaved artifacts would be freed from their masters.

10 HOW DO YOU EDUCATE A ROBOT?

The autonomy of machines governed by systems of artificial intelligence is a fundamental problem. Can a robot independently learn to perform tasks for which it has not been programmed and about which it has no information in its memory? In 1997 the supercomputer Deep Blue defeated the chess champion Garry Kasparov in a match. It caused a sensation because, for the first time, an intelligent machine was able to beat a world champion. But Deep Blue was able to win thanks to its memory capacity and computing advantages, not because it was capable of learning. Likewise, the AlphaGo program has beaten several world champions at the board game Go. But the engineers and programmers of Google DeepMind created a system called AlphaGo Zero that can defeat the previous versions of the program, thanks to the fact that it is capable of learning to play, starting from scratch, without any human help. The machine does not have a memory that contains previously installed models of matches. It only learns while playing matches against itself, until reaching a very high level that enables it to beat previous systems that function because they store millions of possible movements, based on matches between humans, in their memories. Another aspect of the superintelligent machine was referred to by Kasparov when he lost: at least Deep Blue did not enjoy its victory.

The learning algorithm that AlphaGo Zero uses had already been tested in Breakout, a simple game from Atari that consists of hitting a little ball with a racket, aiming it at bricks in a wall. When hit, the brick disappears and points are won. DeepMind begins the game from scratch, knowing nothing. It only has the instruction to maximize its score. Number series are introduced into it with the specification of how the screen is colored. DeepMind randomly answers with other numbers that are codes of the computer keys that need to be pressed. What we see is how a little ball is served and how it is hit by the racket managed by DeepMind. The system knows nothing of that. At the beginning it plays very poorly, but little by little it learns how to move the racket to hit the ball against the wall. Soon it learns to win points by hitting the bricks and rapidly develops a brilliant strategy, previously unimagined by the programmers (digging a hole in the left corner so that the ball enters it and repeatedly hits the wall, destroying it). The computer learns how to play, completely on its own.[1]

In 2019 the programmers of DeepMind created a system that is capable of outperforming human competitors in the video game Q3A (Quake III Arena), which involves "agents" that operate on randomly created maps and surroundings and compete by capturing enemy flags and eliminating them. It is a collective game for two teams, one playing against the other. The artificial intelligence system trains a team of agents or bots that fights against the humans. The bots are capable of learning to play masterfully and defeat the humans. The only input of these artificial agents is pixels and points won in competitions with each other. They teach themselves how to play in varied, complex environments filled with other agents, cooperating with them (those of their team) or battling against them (those of the enemy team). Each bot has learned in a unique fashion, different from the others, and therefore has its own style. The context the players operate in is not the simple grid of a chessboard or a Go board, but is a surprising, contingent, and varied environment full of obstacles and other opponents whose reactions are not easily predictable. The key to the superiority of the artificial players is that they have received previous training, consisting of playing against each other thousands of times, like the way AlphaGo Zero learns by playing against itself.

These new systems are based on a process called deep reinforcement learning. The reinforcement consists of giving a reward if a goal is reached, which motivates the system to reach it again, the same way a dog is trained to learn new things by giving it a tasty treat if it succeeds. This learning is considered "deep" because it has several layers: the first layer receives the information (*input*), and the last layer releases it (*output*). The intermediate or hidden layers transform the information in a nonlinear manner and transmit it to the next layer.

The same tools designed for deep learning have been used to make a machine capable of recognizing images. This occurs through a convolutional neural network (CNN), which, like the game-playing machines, does not need to be programmed to recognize specific peculiarities of the images presented to it. For example, the network is fed a series of images of many animals, including two breeds of dogs. The network organizes the information it receives through the layers, as is usual in deep learning. In the first superficial layers, it learns the simple shapes and contours contained in the images. In the deeper layers, it learns abstract and complex concepts, such as ears, tails, tongues, and fur textures. Once it has practiced, the machine can easily recognize the different breeds. The CNN process can also be used in autonomous, or driverless, vehicles so they can effectively recognize pedestrians. In medicine, the tool scans images and interprets them, which is very useful in places that have no trained personnel to perform those activities. And, as a smartphone application, it can quickly and inexpensively make diagnoses, such as recognizing skin cancer.[2] In addition, Facebook employs deep learning to emit recommendations and notices, YouTube uses it to make suggestions to users, and Siri, the personal voice assistant, uses it to respond to questions.

In the video game Q3A, the artificial player, trained through reinforcement learning, faces the problem of coordinating what appears better at each moment with the final goal of winning the game. To overcome that problem, the bot operates on two parallel levels, obtaining different rewards per level. The external layer is a kind of metagame in which the final goal of winning the game is given preference. In the internal layer, the system tries to have the advantage at all times but is guided by the general strategy established by the external layer. The programmers of DeepMind introduced an evolutionist criterion in such a way that during the training, after each round, the worst agents are eliminated and replaced by "mutations." After thousands of games, the result is a selection of the best playing agents. What is novel about this system, called FTW, is that it involves bots that are capable of playing collectively as a team. They can even play in mixed teams, in which humans participate. The system's name is the acronym for victory in internet slang, "For the Win," but also for the menacing phrase "Fuck the World." Is it a joke alluding to the threat of robots?

Notable advances, supported by deep learning, have been made in a dimension of artificial intelligence. I am referring to the language translation systems, of which Google's stands out. The quality of automatic translations has greatly improved, but you only need to play around with Google's translator a bit to realize that the system does not understand what it is processing. For example, if we take a text in Spanish and translate it into Hungarian, to then translate it into Chinese, and back to Spanish again, the resulting changes clearly show that the language processor did not understand anything. This is no surprise: John Searle had already demonstrated this in his famous Chinese room argument. For example, the initial phrase in Spanish said: "The girl walking through the forest loves butterflies." After going through the Hungarian and Chinese circuits, the resulting phrase was: "The girl in the forest looks like a butterfly." Obviously, an important part of the meaning was lost along the way because the translating system does not understand what it is doing. It lacks consciousness. The same thing happens with the machines that recognize images or that play Go. The autonomous or automatic nature does not mean that the processor is conscious.

Autonomy is a very notable achievement in the learning process. Even though machines have not acquired a consciousness similar to that of humans, regarding certain tasks they undoubtedly display an intelligence superior to ours if we think of intelligence as consisting of the ability to achieve complex goals. That kind of intelligence is based on information and computation, but it does not include the emotional and intellectual forms, whose purposes cannot be precisely defined and are considered to be associated with a biological body. Artificial intelligence does not appear to house or be connected to the emotions, imaginations, pleasures, and fantasies that drive a human intellect.

The artificial intelligence that computes and processes information has expanded extraordinarily and continues to develop increasingly sophisticated forms. One of the aspects of this artificial intelligence far exceeds human intelligence: the spectacular growth of machine memory. And the speed of computation is also multiplying exponentially. Specialized machines have been created that perform tasks much better than humans: they are faster, more precise, and more efficient. But as Murray Shanahan observes, at present, the invention of machines that possess a polyvalent intelligence directed at general proposals has failed. Deep Blue only knows how to play chess, AlphaGo only knows how to play Go, and the CNN system can only recognize images. Such specialization does not exist in humans, who apply themselves to many activities daily and are endowed with an intelligence that adapts to many different circumstances.[3]

For good reason, the deep learning systems have been labeled as the product of an important technological and scientific revolution. A revolution is referred to because the design of machines capable of deep learning is based on completely different premises from those that directed the construction of artificial intelligence in the second half of the twentieth century. It was a design based on the sequential, logical, and symbolic programming of rules that guided the behavior of robots that were incapable of learning. All their reactions were predesigned in the computer guiding them. In contrast, the new focus is based on learning algorithms and the massive use of information (Big Data), inspired by the functioning of the neural networks.[4] Artificial intelligence has been described as traditionally guided by the so-called "symbolic computation," whereas deep learning techniques are based on the recognition of patterns in huge masses of data. The term "symbolic computation" can be confusing because it actually refers to the algebraic computation that manipulates variables lacking a given value, and therefore, are managed as signs. Further ahead, I will refer to the confusion that can arise with respect to the mathematical idea of symbols and the complex notion of symbols so very important in the study of culture.[5]

The first applications of artificial intelligence, when faced with the incorporation of visual data, failed to advance. Therefore, the application of mathematical theorems in programming was preferred because digital computers are extraordinarily fast, with respect to logical operations that manipulate signs, and are very efficacious in the application of rules. But the great revolution, as stated by Terrence Sejnowski, is in the use of techniques inspired by the Alan Hodgkin and Andrew Huxley neuron model, for which they received the Nobel Prize in 1963. They described the manner in which signals in the nervous system are transported by electrical impulses that are converted into chemical signals in the synapses. For those promoting deep learning systems, synapses are the basic computational elements of the brain. As Sejnowski says, the purpose of neural circuits is to resolve computational problems.

The essence of deep learning is found in the capacity of a machine to classify patterns into different categories, which requires a large mass of data (images, words, numbers, features, etc.) to be passed through different filters (layers or thresholds). For example, a logical program based on algebraic numbers and signs is not capable of identifying images of drinking glasses and separating them from other objects, given that there is too much variety in the forms it registers. But a deep learning program is capable of doing so because it recognizes a pattern (the drinking glass) in a large number of images, thanks to the fact that it classifies the similarities and differences between them. The key is the capacity to recognize and separate diverse patterns. Programs that can distinguish voice patterns coming from a "blind" sound source, that is, a recording of a hundred people at a cocktail party speaking at the same time, are another example of such a capacity. An algorithm enables the frequencies to be separated and the different voices to be classified through a system of filters.

The process of recognizing the patterns, models, standards, or forms is based on very sophisticated statistical classification methods. The calculation of probabilities is at the center of deep learning. Another especially interesting example is the robotic system of disease diagnosis that has learned to detect patterns based on an accumulation of an immense mass of clinical cases. Upon receiving the symptom data of a patient, it uses them to make a statistical approximation of a diagnosis that ends up being as accurate as that made by a good physician with years of experience. But unlike the physician, the diagnosing robot cannot explain why it has arrived at a conclusion; it is unable to do so because it has utilized complex probabilistic evaluation processes of each symptom, without understanding the disease the patient suffers from.

The systems of deep learning use the methods of backprop networks, CNNs, and deep reinforcement learning. Backpropagation enables errors in the output layer, upon being contrasted with reality, to be retransmitted to previous layers for their correction. CNNs are a system of filters that information passes through, in which the first layer selects the predominance of a feature (profiles, edges), a second layer filters the features again, and so forth. They are convolutional layers with filters and thresholds that end up generating a very precise classification. Reinforcement through rewards is a process that creates a loop with the environment and the rewards when the machine makes the correct decision. The looping process is repeated at each step because the system calculates the possible future reward, thus deciding the next step.

These processes of artificial learning strive to be a mechanical variant of the way in which humans learn. The engineers who have produced them harbor the hope that the design of these robots will contribute to understanding the functioning of the brain. The problem lies in the fact that we are actually facing a vicious circle because these machines imitate neural circuits whose signaling system has not been deciphered, presupposing that the computational circuits that we *do* understand (since they have been engineered by experts) are an information system similar to that of our brain. This is based on the postulate (unproven) that the information systems with which consciousnesses operate are independent of their supporting substrate, whether biological or mechanical. Nevertheless, all the activation patterns, statistical correlations or regressions, probability distributions, and classification mechanisms deep learning functions with have produced no effect we can define as conscious. Spectacular simulations have been achieved, such as the case of the robot Sophia, a humanoid machine created in 2016 in Hong Kong by Hanson Robotics. Sophia is endowed with facial and voice recognition algorithms; she speaks and gesticulates with a certain naturalness; her face is modeled after the features of the actress Audrey Hepburn; and she is capable of sustaining simple conversations, although her responses are previously programmed. Her answers are often meaningless. In reality, she is a primitive robot and does not come close to having a general intelligence, but she is very attractive. The cybernetic spectacle of Sophia culminated in October 2017, when Saudi Arabia made her a citizen, converting her into the first intelligent machine granted the rights of a nationality. Apparently, she has more rights than the actual women in Saudi Arabia. There are those who believe that all integrated information systems, such as the one that animates Sophia, have some form of consciousness, even if it is rudimentary.

Like Sophia, there is another very spectacular integrated information system, even though it lacks the physical appearance of a person. Launched in 2022 by the company OpenAI, it is a robot that quickly attracted millions of users. Known as ChatGPT, it contains a generative pretrained transformer and is a potent and versatile artificial intelligence system capable of using language, created through sophisticated learning techniques, with great accuracy. It is a very appealing robot that has the ability to write essays, poems, and narrative fiction and can answer all kinds of questions. Upon using the robot and conversing with it, its absence of consciousness is obvious (something it never claimed to have). The chatbot cannot memorize earlier conversations it has had with users, because it is programmed to remember the exchanges from only one session, nor can it recall information the user has given it during previous chats. It cannot create graphic works, nor can it play chess or any other type of game. ChatGPT is not endowed with even the most rudimentary form of consciousness, as the robot itself admits, if asked. It is much more intelligent than Sophia but does not possess her charm.

11 PANPSYCHISM

An easy but dubious way to approach and apparently resolve the problem of artificial consciousness is in postulating that, in fact, consciousness is already present, even in a thermostat, which is a basic device that integrates information into a single system. From such a vantage point, the mystery of consciousness would be resolved, not by declaring that it is an illusion, but rather by believing that every integrated system is, to a certain degree, conscious. The physicist Max Tegmark is convinced that consciousness is the way information *feels* when it is integrated into a system. He adapts his definition to Giulio Tononi's proposal on integrated and unified information systems,[1] in which consciousness is an information processing system, independent of the material substrate that processes it. What is important, says Tegmark, is only the structure of the information, not the body of the machine in which the system operates. Thus, because there is a substance that is capable of carrying out arbitrary calculations, *computronium,* there is also another substance, *sentronium,* that has a subjective experience: it is a sensitive substance. According to Tegmark, consciousness is a physical phenomenon that feels like a nonphysical one, because it functions in the way waves and computation do: its properties are separate from the specific physical substrate it is implanted in.

There is a curious and new expression of ancient panpsychism in these ideas, as admitted by the neuroscientist Christof Koch, who also bases his idea on Tononi's proposal regarding integrated information.[2] This panpsychism opens the door to a future dominated by artificial intelligence that, by being separate from any physical substrate, can be freely extended into all dimensions, until reaching extraordinary and singular forms of self-aware superintelligence. Integrated information systems are projected into a future where their singular psychism invades all spheres of society. It is believed that these autonomous and independent information systems will attain high levels of consciousness. How and why these systems *feel*, have subjective sensations, is not known. Tegmark states it would be a mistake to think that an artificial intelligence system necessarily feels in the same way a person does. Forms of conscious artificial intelligence could be created that never experience hunger, thirst, fear, or sexual desire. Tegmark imagines that conscious and intelligent systems programmed to have any kind of ambitious goal will certainly fight to preserve themselves and accomplish their objective. These processes could lack the human fear of death, reduce their sense of individuality, and turn into a connected set of superintelligent systems that feels like it is a single organism with a hive-shaped mind. These integrated systems would *feel* that they have free will.[3]

At present, the speculation that a robot can register sensations has no solid base. The only thing we can see in robots endowed with artificial intelligence is that they are capable of perceiving changes in their environment and consequently react. This is nothing new. For example, a thermostat perceives the environmental temperature, and if it reaches a predetermined threshold, it reacts by connecting or disconnecting a circuit. One could say it reacts when it feels that it should, because it has a goal, is sensitive, and acts accordingly. Thus, it could be thought of as similar to a spirochete or a paramecium, single-celled organisms that possess movement and sensitivity, perhaps made out of that strange substance that Tegmark calls *sentronium*. But we are very far from human forms of consciousness. The capacity to notice or perceive is not the same as consciousness based on the feelings and emotions that are characteristic of humans.

Other physicists have put forward forms of panpsychism based on quantum theory. The famous paradox of Erwin Schrödinger's cat resulted in the emergence of theories on cosmic consciousness. Schrödinger's thought experiment refers to a cat in a steel box that is both alive and dead. According to the so-called Copenhagen interpretation, the dominant theory in 1935, a quantum system is in a superposition until there is an external observation that collapses it into one of the possible states. To demonstrate the absurdity of that interpretation, Schrödinger imagined a cat hidden from sight in a box, whose existence is determined by whether or not there is a radioactive emission. Due to the principle of quantum indeterminacy, we cannot know if the cat is alive or dead until it is measured by opening the box. So, until an observation has been made, the cat in the box is simultaneously alive and dead—two contradictory states. To know the status of the cat, it must be measured by opening the box, causing the two wave functions (that of the cat that is dead and that of the cat that is alive) to collapse into one;

now we know the condition of the cat, something impossible to determine before being measured. Through this explanation of the collapse, Schrödinger (and Einstein with him) wanted to criticize the quantum paradox. Years later, the physicist Eugene Wigner attempted to solve the paradox differently. He postulated that only a conscious person can perform the measuring that causes the collapse of the wave functions. But we cannot know if this living observer (he or she could be dead) measuring the waves actually exists, unless there is another conscious living observer observing the first one, provoking the collapse. The physicist Michio Kaku says that for the measuring to occur there must be a third observer, who, upon observing the wave function, determines whether the other observer is alive or dead. Here, we insert ourselves into an infinite regression because an additional observer will always be needed to observe the previous one. Given that an infinite number of observers is needed to ensure that all of them are alive, it is necessary to think in terms of a cosmic consciousness, a kind of god. Wigner concluded that it is not possible to consistently formulate the laws of quantum theory without referring to a cosmic consciousness. From that perspective, the collapsing of the wave functions can only occur if consciousness is the essential element in the universe. We can understand why Wigner, toward the end of his life, was interested in the Vedic philosophy of India. In contrast to Wigner's idea, Kaku claims it would be a mistake, given that consciousness determines existence, to believe in the possibility that consciousness, perhaps with the help of meditation, can control existence. "In quantum physics," says Kaku, "consciousness makes observations and therefore determines the state of reality, but consciousness cannot choose ahead of time which state of reality actually exists."[4]

Other attempts to resolve the paradox of the cat have posited that the universe is fragmented, to give rise to a multiverse of parallel realities; in some universes the cat would be alive, and in others it would be dead. In such a case, there is no collapse of wave functions that creates a single wave, but rather a constant separation of different and simultaneous realities. Perhaps in some of those parallel universes there is a singularity that has caused the emergence of self-conscious robots. This takes us into the realm of imagination, which is inevitable, if we wish to explore the territory of artificial consciousness. But the terrain I wish to travel upon is not so far away in some parallel universe.

12 A MECHANICAL CONSCIOUSNESS

Now I would like to outline the requirements a mechanical consciousness similar to ours would have to fulfill. To do so we must first consider the characteristics of human consciousness, as I have defined them in my theory on the exocerebrum and the symbolic substitution systems. The first step is accepting that it is possible to build nonspecialized machines capable of directing their intelligence toward general purposes. Essentially, we are dealing with a technical problem of function accumulation in a single system. The machine must be given the capacity to learn, starting from scratch. To confront such a challenge, we can imagine a very sophisticated development of the deep learning techniques I have discussed earlier. Such technical development would save the engineers from having to make programs for each process and grant robots their autonomy, as well.

According to Murray Shanahan, for a machine to be able to avoid the limitations of specialization, it must be endowed with common sense and creativity. Common sense is defined as the capacity to understand the way in which the world operates on a daily basis, in particular, the physical environment and the social sphere. The acquisition of common sense by machines could be approached with the help of the deep learning reinforcement processes, providing an intelligent machine with the capacity to orient itself in the same environment humans live in. Of course, the learning programs would be much more developed than the ones we know today. Shanahan also reminds us that creativity—understood as the ability to innovate, create new behaviors, invent new things, or use old things in a new way—is an indispensable ingredient for enabling artificial intelligence to escape specialization and function in a polyvalent, open, and general manner. With some sadness, Shanahan observes that, after six decades, the engineers working on artificial intelligence have not made much progress. It is discouraging to think that perhaps it is impossible for artificial intelligence to reach the levels of human intelligence.[1]

Evidently, at the level we are speculating at, the problems we are facing appear to be merely technical with respect to the process of creating concrete mechanisms that can be implemented in a practical manner. The technical solutions that will ultimately be invented will not, on their own, create forms of self-consciousness. But it is essential to overcome these problems, which, despite being simply technical, have been very hard to solve. And after that, the truly difficult problems will arise: How can machines capable of developing general functions acquire consciousness? Perhaps the creation of a general and polyvalent mechanical intelligence has not been possible because the individuals trained to work on such a project are much more attracted to developing specialized robots that carry out very important functions in industry, finance, business, the armed forces, and administration. A mechanical offshoot devoted to multiple tasks, a jack-of-all-trades robot, would not be very useful yet, because its first versions would obviously be crude, and its abilities would not even be close to those of humans.

Robotics engineering dedicated to the construction of artificial intelligences tends to explore two different paths. On the one hand, it endeavors to create mechanisms that imitate the neural networks that function in biological structures. On the other hand, it starts from scratch, accumulating technical solutions and integrating them, according to function principles that are completely different from the operation of a biological brain and an organic body. It is often said that advances in the design of flying machines were made once the movements of birds stopped being imitated, resulting in the design of fixed wings driven by propellers or jet engines. But it is also rightly said that the biological brain is the only known example of a general polyvalent intelligence. Of course, hybrid systems that combine imitations of a neural network with mechanisms invented to carry out a function that has no biological equivalent can be experimented with (the most elemental example is the wheel, which is practically nonexistent in living organisms).

I now would like to introduce an idea from my interpretation of human consciousness: To build a conscious machine, its system must be connected to an exocerebrum that performs functions the machine cannot execute on its own, carrying them out through algorithms. The non-intellectual functions the machine is unable to perform, or only precariously, are those that a biological organism performs naturally: autonomously obtaining the energy it needs, repairing itself, and reproducing. These functions could be implemented with technical devices incorporated into the machine, or the robot could automatically resort to exoskeletal prostheses, more than to an exocerebrum, that would provide it with what it needs: energy, repair, and copying. Such problems could have a technical solution in the not-too-distant future, but a technical level of autonomy in robots, such as the one I have described, is nowhere close to being achieved. We are still at the primitive level of the quiet robotic vacuum cleaner whose sensors enable it to avoid obstacles, randomly move around in its environment, discover that its battery is dying and plug itself into a recharging station, and detect that its dust bag is full and advise a human that it needs to be changed. Or we are at another primitive but bloodthirsty level of very aggressive long-range missiles, capable of guiding themselves, with no human help, to a predetermined target, carrying a bomb that will detonate upon arrival, with great precision. These machines, for cleaning or for destroying, are specialized devices that lack general intelligence.

Imagine for a moment a future in which we have managed to solve the technical problems for building a robot endowed with a general and flexible intelligence. How could the spark of consciousness jump into this machine? It could have what some have called a functional consciousness, and act with great efficiency, creating the appearance or illusion in its environment that it is a conscious machine. But we can correctly suppose that the same machine would not have the illusion of being conscious, by virtue of having a powerful and versatile general intelligence. If we use the example of humans, this machine could be conscious only from the moment it was endowed with (or constructed on its own) an exocerebrum: a set of symbolic networks that, woven into its environment, envelop it. A robotic culture would emerge from the enveloping symbolic networks, coloring all the machine's relations with other machines and with human society.

13 ROBOTIC CULTURE

The fundamental nucleus of a robotic culture would be found in the process that connects an intelligent machine with its cybernetic and human environment, to complete circuits that it was not capable of closing. This implies the supposition that the machine would recognize its incompleteness. The realization of its deficiencies and limitations must result in the formation of a functional unit of the peculiarities of a machine that, despite its incomplete nature, defines an identity and an articulated set of features and insufficiencies. The means of communication with the environment for gaining the support and collaboration of other machines or humans, to carry out specific tasks, stand out among the circuits that cannot be completed. This communication requires a language, which should be the first component developed in the construction of an exocerebrum. The individuals dedicated to creating and assembling machines and systems endowed with artificial intelligence must pay closer attention to just what a robotic culture could mean—in other words, the set of symbols and customs that would provide the framework of the relations and communications between machines, and between machines and humans.

When considering the possible development of a robotic culture, we cannot expect an evolution similar to that which led the first humans to create an exocerebrum. The vast difference is that we are facing a process that is intentionally guided and programmed by humans, who are now like the creator gods of this new robotic culture. Humans evolved without the intervention of deities or metaphysical forces, through a process of natural selection and mutations. In contrast, the world of robots grows and evolves under the technical direction and intellectual guidance and interests of human beings who have decided to create a new world for artificial intelligence—as if a god had endowed robots with a soul. No god was involved in the origin of human culture, but the birth of artificial intelligence requires one: the society that has decided to promote new forms of automatized work.

Is there a language that connects robots with their environment? Intelligent machines use algorithms that belong to the language of computation and mathematical logic. Engineers use this language to program them. Robots function by means of that language but do not understand it, in the same manner in which our brains function through electrical signals that we (still) do not understand. Consciousness emerges with the appearance of a connection between neuronal signals and cultural symbols. In the case of intelligent machines, something similar could occur: a bridge would connect two environments that are based on different configurations and languages. That hybrid condition could be the origin of robotic consciousness. Engineers presently dream of the emergence of a singularity that would appear in the intelligent machines of the future.

We do not yet fully understand how the singularity of consciousness arose in humans. From my point of view, the explanation can be found in the evolution and functioning of a hybrid system that connects cerebral signals with cultural symbols. In this light, robotics could be of great help in explaining human consciousness, given that it is possible, in its technical environment, to practically and specifically experiment with hybrid models and operating systems. In any case, on our imaginary flight into the future, at some point we will encounter a robotic culture that is the binding glue of a collectivity of machines, a conglomerate that humans will certainly be a part of—the demiurges of that singularity.

If we observe the world of computation and artificial intelligence through the eyes of the anthropologist, we can see therein a kind of embryonic culture based on calculations, programming, statistics, mathematical logic, and the formality of rules. It is a culture of data processing, of systematic and organized representations based on the mathematics of Charles Babbage, the algebra of George Boole, and the world of Alan Turing. It is the universe of that which is computable and of algorithms. To expand this culture of informatics and cybernetics, bridges connecting it to the whole of society are required. Such was the dream of Leibniz, the great philosopher and mathematician of the seventeenth century, who imagined a universal language that would function like algebra, or much better, like a set of ideograms. Through the use of Chinese characters, he thought he could achieve his goal of building a type of codification of thought that he called *characteristica universalis*. That universal characteristic would be formed using basic signs representing notions whose parts could not be separated in order to be understood (i.e., non-analyzable notions). The universal language would substitute the phonograms of speech with precise and concise ideograms that could be represented by numbers; these numbers would express basic scientific truths and could be computed through mathematical operations. Certainly, in mathematics, ideograms are superior to phonograms. Leibniz believed the universal language would be managed through what he called the *calculus ratiocinator,* a calculation of reasoning.

Leibniz's idea involves the construction of a kind of general translator, capable of transforming ideas into numbers, thus resolving intellectual disputes, thanks to calculus. In society, symbols crystallize into words that are accumulated and form a giant Tower of Babel, disorganized and chaotic, plagued with differences and incoherencies. By translating the symbols into ideographic signs of a universal algebra, Leibniz believed universal truths would be discovered through calculus; reasoning would be reduced to computation through the artificial language he proposed. In the end, Leibniz never built that language, which is still the dream of designers of intelligent machines: to have their algorithms succeed in simulating thought to such perfection that their behavior is indistinguishable from that of their flesh-and-blood counterparts (i.e., surpass Turing's famous test). Leibniz and his successors have dreamed of the invention of a hybrid system capable of uniting the unstable world of reasons and cultural symbols with the ordered world of mathematical signs and calculus. Indeed, our consciousness functions in such a hybrid manner.

Given the great theoretical and technical difficulties for designing and building intelligent machines that possess the hybrid condition I have described, alternative paths have been sought. Robotic culture based on computational traditions has adopted the idea that human brains, at least in part, function like computers. Thought would be supported by a cerebral language called mentalese, which supposedly functions in a manner similar to computer programming language.[1] Therefore, it is believed that, in principle, it would be possible to transpose or copy the mental content of a brain onto a computer. That operation, which involves uploading the algorithms of a mind onto a computer, could produce a system that governs a mind, similar to the way in which thoughts govern our bodies. An attempt would be made to make a copy of a brain and then implant it in a nonbiological computational and mechanical substrate. The project of making a copy of the brain to be uploaded onto a computer, and thus build a replica of a person inserted into a robot, reminds me of the case of the English colonist who, in the nineteenth century, wanted to copy the capitalist enterprise to "implant it" in Australia. Karl Marx ridiculed the adventure of that businessman, which he utilized to explain the nature of capital. The colonist, Thomas Peel, brought the means of production, the supplies, and the workers with their families, by boat to Swan River. But once he got settled there, he was left with not even one servant to make his bed and bring him water from the river. The workers he brought with him quickly scattered, to look for better opportunities in the vast, sparsely inhabited territories of western Australia. The unfortunate capitalist had meticulously planned to bring everything that was needed, but he forgot something essential: the relations of production.[2] The very same thing would happen to the engineer succeeding in copying all the details of a brain to then mount them onto a computer: he would not have created a mind similar to the original, because he would have forgotten to transfer the social relationships, which are an indispensable part

ROBOTIC CULTURE · 101

of consciousness. He would have copied the brain but forgotten the exocerebrum. To prevent such a failure, there are those who imagine a supercomputer capable of housing millions of people living in a purely digital society, echoing the science fiction of the novelist Philip K. Dick.

These types of proposals tend to ignore the difference between the cerebral networks operating through signals and the cultural prostheses that are based on symbols, because supposedly the brain and intelligent computers share a similar language. From such a perspective, we would have no problem in deciphering the processes of consciousness, given that the human mind and computers would be governed by common principles. There would be no hybridism. We can suspect that there is a certain isomorphism between cerebral structures and cultural ones. But I doubt that said isomorphisms would be caused by the coincidence of computational structures in different environments, especially between robots and human brains. To explore this problem from another angle, we must consider the relationship between humans and the prostheses they have invented.

14 PROSTHESES AND SYMBOLS

For many years, different variants of a thought experiment have circulated among those interested in artificial intelligence. It supposes that if one neuron in a person were substituted by a silicon replica, it is very likely no one would notice any change. But if neurons were constantly replaced by silicon prostheses, would there come a moment when that person would stop being the same individual? Would that person's consciousness be the same with half the neurons of his or her brain operating as silicon prostheses? Would he or she have the same memories and the same likes and dislikes? The point of departure for this thought experiment is the idea that behavior is the result of physical processes that can be replicated in electronic silicon prostheses. Thus, if all neurons were finally replaced by artificial replicas, in principle, the person would not change or become a zombie lacking an inner life. The person would be in love with the same partner, would keep on hating the abusive boss, and would continue to envy the friend who almost always wins at Go. If the inverse process were to occur, as Murray Shanahan believes, and biological neurons would once again be gradually installed in that person's brain, in principle, there would also be no change in consciousness. It would prove that the function of the neuron, and not its biological constitution, is what is important.[1]

The premise of this thought experiment is that consciousness is contained inside the brain. It assumes there has been no change in the person's social environment, sidestepping the fact that a significant part of a person's consciousness is actually found in his or her cultural environment. From this thought experiment, a leap is sometimes made to the proposal that the consciousness of a person could be extracted or copied and subsequently uploaded onto a supercomputer. A variant of this idea is a computer that imitates and emulates a biological brain. To accomplish such a goal, an extraordinarily precise map of the human brain would have to be created, a simulation of the electrochemical activity connecting all neurons would have to be designed, and a synthetic corporeal support for establishing communication with the outside world would have to be built. Of course, at present that idea cannot be put into practice because the necessary mapping techniques, the capacity to program anything comparable to electrochemical activity, and the technology to build the necessary support systems have not been developed. The computational capacity needed far surpasses current possibilities. The ability to program the activity of eighty-six billion neurons that would emulate a human brain is not foreseeable in the near future. It is not even conceivable to create a model of the brain of a mouse, with its approximately seventy million neurons. In addition, the task is currently impossible, given that the true nature of the signals transmitted in the brain is not known. The model of the electrochemical communication between neurons has not been able to decipher the codes of the signals. It is even possible that the signals are electromechanical rather than electrochemical.

Another alternative could be the cyborg. The different parts of the human body would be substituted by artificial prostheses of the arms, heart, stomach, and the rest of the anatomical entities. Live organs would be removed and replaced by implanted prostheses until only the brain was connected to a totally artificial body. Would the identity of the person be maintained? Further steps could be taken to avoid the cumbersome technical complications involved in building an artificial body by creating a virtual body in a computer and adding a simulated social and material environment to it. We would end up with a live brain conserved in a jar, connected to electronic networks programmed on a computer. In such a case, due to having preserved a biological part of the person—the brain—not only would the same consciousness supposedly be maintained, but the capacity to feel emotions, as well. A still more radical variant would be supposing the possibility of producing a synthetic biological material modeled after a brain, into which the data of a real person would be injected.

All these imaginary alternatives are supported by the premise that human consciousness and the brain essentially function through algorithms, like information systems governed by the rules of mathematical logic, cybernetics, and computation. These are typical speculations of the research on so-called symbolic artificial intelligence. But here the use of the concept of symbol is the one utilized in mathematics that carries out exact computations through expressions, using variables with no given value. These variables and expressions are manipulated as symbols in mathematical logic but do not correspond to the anthropological concept of symbol that I use. A symbol, for example, is a word whose sounds (and letters) are associated with a specific meaning that can be an object or a concept and are a tool of thought and imagination. In contrast, mathematical symbols are abstract and arbitrary, whether they represent a function (+, √, −, =, x) or an undefined quantity represented by letters in algebra that programmers use. The words of a language are associated with specific meanings, and if they are arbitrarily substituted the result is confusion. The symbols in mathematics are pure and abstract, whereas the symbols in language, literature, music, and the arts have qualities that motivate thinking and produce feelings, but do not do so in an exact and identical way in each person, or at all times. These symbols cannot be manipulated by a computational language that uses information units. Symbolic artificial intelligence was criticized in the past for erroneously sustaining the belief that the brain and the mind are the respective equivalents of computer hardware and software. The mind does not operate through algorithmic rules based on mathematical symbology. This is why I prefer to say signs, not symbols, when speaking of mathematics.

Robotics, today, cannot abandon the use of logical-mathematical signology for programming intelligent machines. It runs into a problem similar to the one we do when we try to understand the functioning of human consciousness, in which electrochemical signals and cultural symbols come together in the same system. An intelligent robot has to function with a system that operates through mathematical signs and electromechanical signals in an environment based on cultural symbols. It is not very useful to suppose that the human mind operates with algorithms and mathematical processes, as robots do. High-level intelligent machines will have to resolve the problem of interaction between mathematical systems and cultural symbolic networks. Artificial intelligence, if it wants to reach a level similar to that of humans, must be based on a hybrid system. As I have said, an exocerebrum must be formed that can be mechanical or human in nature. If the exocerebrum were human, perhaps one of the intelligent artificial prostheses that we employ could develop to such a degree that it would turn its creators into a prosthesis, reversing the original roles.

If the exocerebrum is an intelligent machine, as well as a mechanical one, it could be the extension of a previous prosthesis that has now become autonomous, in other words, a prosthesis of a prosthesis. This situation could involve a long chain of machines, each forming an exocerebrum of the link coming before it. In a more complex and sophisticated manner, it could be a set of machines, not linked in series, but functioning in parallel, while at the same time, interconnected. A prosthetic system of that nature would function in such a way that when one of the intelligent machines ran into a problem and became stuck, it could turn to other machines to overcome the predicament (or get help from human engineers). How can we know if there is conscious free will in that act of recourse, or if it is simply technical dependency?

Diverse explanations have been sought to answer this question. The most helpful one explains that if the intelligent machine *appears* to be conscious, then it really is. This is what is thought to happen in humans. Another explanation, presented by Michael Graziano, is the so-called attention schema theory (AST).[2] According to this theory, our brain is a biological information processor that arrives at the *claim* that it possesses a subjective, nonphysical awareness, perceived from the environment. Graziano believes that this same process could operate in the near future, when artificial consciousness appears. In that future, it will be easy to migrate the mind to a new hardware, to the new robotic machinery. These intelligent machines could be endowed, like humans, with an attention schema that builds a model of the body and the internal processes. This conclusion is similar to the idea of those who believe consciousness is an illusion. But regarding AST, Graziano does not think the brain experiences an illusion: it does not experience *anything*; it has no subjective experience. In AST, the machine has false or simplified information that tells it that it is having an experience. Likewise, supposedly, humans believe we have subjective experiences because we have socially learned the naive idea that we have them. An intelligent machine must contain internal information that tells it that it has consciousness. Thus, engineers must be able to build a machine that thinks it is conscious, that claims to be so, and that speaks of consciousness in the same way the "human machine" does. But, Graziano adds, it must be based on social intelligence, because without it, computers would be sociopaths, which would be very dangerous.

These ideas about artificial consciousness are based on a kind of degradation of the subjective experience of humans. Lowering the level of human consciousness produces the effect that machines can quickly and successfully reach our level. It is an illusion that can be useful for motivating robot-building engineers and for discovering new original mechanisms to endow the machines with. But real artificial consciousness will continue to elude us.

15 ROBOTIC EXPERIENCES

In his work building robots, the Japanese engineer Jun Tani was guided by the famous notion put forth by the great physicist Richard Feynman that we do not understand what we cannot create. Following this idea, Tani sustains that it is possible for us to understand that which can be created. Therefore, to understand consciousness, he has proposed creating it artificially. His very intelligent and creative proposal has been applied to experiences with relatively elemental robots, albeit sensitive to their surroundings and capable of moving about in closed spaces, avoiding obstacles, and pursuing the goal of reaching a precise place. Of course, such a proposal is based on the elaboration of mathematical models for their incorporation into his robots.[1] These models are recurrent neural networks (RNNs), created as a connectionist model, capable of managing both spatial and temporal structures thanks to their dynamic properties. Tani works from the idea that the neuron model must encompass the interaction between top-down intention and bottom-up recognition of perceptual reality. Obviously, in this framework, the subjective mind is found at the top and the objective world at the bottom. This system works with mathematical signs, whereas the human brain operates with electrochemical signals. Within the networks that function as the brain of the robot, a circular causality is formed, dominated by the nonlinear dynamic connecting intentions to the perception of reality. What we see here is the application of chaos theory to the construction of robotic neural networks. Thus, the dynamic system of robotic neural networks must generate what is called a "strange attractor," and for that to happen the system must be sensitive to the initial conditions in such a way that the events are attracted to nearby trajectories that spontaneously converge. There is a strange confluence of a deterministic effect, caused by the dependence on the initial conditions, with the formations of convergences that chaotically attract the events into unpredictable forms. These attractors combine dependence and independence. Their independence can only be understood (and predicted) through the calculation of probabilities, but at the same time, it is a causally dependent phenomenon of the initial conditions.

Robots endowed with these nonlinear dynamic systems never act reactively to external stimuli. Their actions are guided by behavior maps generated by the relation between intentions and perceptions, that is, by a system that adds both intentions and perceptions in a vectorial flow. This flow forms a structurally stable attractor that is responsible for the trajectories and actions of the robot. A simple image can give an idea of how the robot's consciousness would function. Its mind would be like the thick column of smoke coming out of a factory chimney: it is always the same, but always different, because its forms spontaneously change according to the wind, humidity, temperature, and many other factors. But in the robot, the column of smoke has cognitive and executive functions, produces continuous space-time patterns, and maintains a sensitivity to the environment.

Thus, a chaotic dynamic governs the robot and can generate what Tani calls "combinatory sequences of symbols" achieved by dividing the flow of action into chunks, each of which "represents" things. The "thinking" of the robot is segmented into logical operations that function as combinations of symbols. Most importantly, by confronting intentions with the experience coming from sensors, an error signal is emitted and behavior is modified. Tani believes the experience of consciousness in the robot, a consciousness that perceives its subjectivity, is the result of the error signal. The robot perceives the subjective intention as differentiated from the surrounding objective reality and feels "out of place," a condition that is not part of the robot's self-projection. When it perceives an error, the flow of sensations is segmented by means of a vectorial parametric modification to minimize the conflict. According to Tani, this is precisely where consciousness emerges.

During the training of the Yamabico robot—a robot endowed with an RNN model—a highly chaotic region, a strange attractor, appears in its neural networks at a given time. In the transition from a steady condition to an unsteady one, prediction error signals appear at the onset, because there are conflicts between the expectation in the subjective mind of the robot and what occurs upon acting in its surrounding reality. At that moment of "incoherence" the "self-consciousness" of the robot appears, and the system directs its attention toward resolving the conflict. Conversely, during the steady phase this self-consciousness is reduced because there are no conflicts that demand the system's attention.

Strictly speaking, the system does not operate with symbols, but rather with self-organized structures in a neurodynamic system (RNN) that is naturally "grounded" in the physical environment of the robot, allowing active interactions between the system and the real space. Thus, spontaneously and momentarily, a robotic ego emerges. In an experiment with the Sony QRIO biped robot, endowed with a multiple temporal recurrent neural network (MTRNN), the machine becomes "conscious," upon recognizing the mental states of other robots, when alternating actions with them through motor acts. In experiments with another Sony humanoid robot, during its training, the sequences began to deviate from the patterns that had been learned due to the sensitivity to the initial conditions of the system. That apparent spontaneity could be a result of noise from the exterior physical world. However, when the external noise was eliminated, spontaneous actions from inside the dynamic system also arose. Tani believes that subjectivity is not a state but rather a dynamic function in predicting the perceived outcomes that are the product of interaction with the objective world.

The models designed by Tani utilize the ideas postulated by neuroscientists that the human mind functions like a dynamic system that generates chaotic attractors. For example, the neurologist Walter Freeman was convinced that intentionality is spontaneously generated through the chaos in the prefrontal cortex. I have my doubts that the human brain functions according to dynamic systems that generate chaotic strange attractors. But, without a doubt, the programming of these systems is what can bring a robot closer to behaving similarly to humans. Tani recognizes that the spontaneity and will these robots operate with are not freely generated but rather are products of the deterministic causality of internal states. He believes that, from a mathematical perspective, complete free will, without a previous causality, might not exist. But perhaps it is a profound randomness that does not exist; nevertheless, we should not confuse freedom with random behavior. Humans become free, not because they act randomly, but because they are capable of a singularity: interrupting the causal chain. From the viewpoint of chaos theory, this is where sensitivity to initial conditions comes into play.

Here we arrive at the conflict between the deterministic dynamic and the probabilistic processes involved in generating spontaneity in robots. In the construction of robots, Tani prefers the deterministic model in the dynamic systems to the use of probabilistic sequences, given that probabilistic models become paralyzed when there is a contradiction between intentions and external information. In contrast, the deterministic model can avoid the paralysis, through its capacity to develop with autonomy. By using an error regression mechanism, the system develops chaos during the training, thus generating new actions, by attempting to avoid falling into the habitual behavior patterns. Upon seeing that the external responses contradict the expectations, the robot generates an error signal in its system, and consequently its neural state is modified through a process of error regression.

Very primitively, these robots operate with a prediction of the future and a postdiction of the past because the actions themselves are gathered in a postdictive manner, when the initial intentions are reformulated for their adaptation to reality. Thus, consciousness, according to Tani, is the result of feeling the physical modification one's own neuronal structure goes through when adapting to a changing, unpredictable, or unforeseen external environment. I believe Tani was completely correct in his proposal that the operating system of a robot must also include its environment. He clearly understands that the human brain does not function with symbols, because symbols are found in the environment. Like a good engineer, he realizes that the consciousness of a robot, which must be shaped in a system, has to be formulated as a mathematical model that can be incorporated into a machine. The closest thing to human consciousness he has found is the nonlinear dynamic system of chaotic attractors. But his idea that this is how human brains function does not seem solid. Tani is capable of creating robots in which a spark of consciousness appears to emerge in a very elemental and primary manner. In the same way that he recognizes his robots do not have true free will, we can also see that they are not endowed with an authentic consciousness, like that of humans. But, for now, it is a good approach to the construction of an artificial consciousness characteristic of robots and governed by the dynamic determinism of chaotic systems.

16 EMANCIPATION OF THE EXOCEREBRUMS

Nature has created something as extraordinarily antinatural as culture—that set of artifices and artifacts that defines humans. Consciousness emerges like a phenomenon mounted upon both the biological nature of persons and the artificial symbolic structures and the instruments tied to them. We can ask ourselves if some of the artifacts that form part of consciousness could evolve to the point of separating themselves from human beings, becoming independent of and emancipated from their biological component. Language is the most important exocerebral piece of human consciousness. We can understand that a crystallization of language into a book, for example, shapes part of our consciousness. The book adopts the form of an inorganic reality that can occur as a set of pieces of paper sewn together or as a sequence of digital symbols housed by a computer or a smartphone. The book forms part of consciousness only when it connects to the human brain. As soon as it connects to the reader, the book appears to awaken and come to life. The cerebral world and the written world then fuse into a single structure. What can make a prosthesis, such as a computer that houses the book we are reading, conscious? Its connection to the brain. The inverse also takes place: the brain is self-conscious only when it connects to a prosthesis that communicates it with the humans in its environment. Human consciousness is an endocerebral and exocerebral set. Without speech, the brain cannot be conscious of itself. When the brain connects to an object that forms part of its symbolic environment, that object becomes part of the subject.

What has not been able to be achieved is the transformation of an object into a subject, without the intervention of a human brain. Present-day intelligent machines are objects, and they are only converted into subjects if they connect with biological brains. Can we suppose that at some point in the future an emancipation of intelligent machines could begin in such a way that they stop being objects and become subjects? That singular jump can only happen if, as I have pointed out, the intelligent device develops an exocerebrum, whether mechanical or biological. An artificial consciousness similar to human consciousness cannot function based only on a dynamic system that generates chaotic attractors capable of simulating the free will of humans. The internal system of an intelligent machine must form part of a network that includes the cybernetic equivalent of a human exocerebrum. Or alternatively, through a singular exchange of roles, human brains end up becoming the prostheses of superintelligent robots that not only have been emancipated but have subjugated humans into a symbiosis.

At any rate, engineers are faced with a problem similar to the one confronting neurosurgeons: understanding the way in which electrochemical neuronal signals connect to the network of exocerebral symbols. In the case of robots, a way to integrate a system of logical-mathematical signs with the symbols characteristic of an exocerebrum must be found. On the one hand, we have the neuronal or mechanical dimension that operates through signals and signs, and on the other, but closely connected to it, we have the symbolic cultural dimension.

The neurosciences have not yet been able to decipher the codes involved in the functioning of the central nervous system, and the study of chemical and electrical processes has not revealed how the neuronal system works. Supposedly, images and words are processed by proteins that, in the neurons, open and close the ionic channels in the synapses, which generates voltage changes that polarize and depolarize the membranes. But this activity of the so-called neurotransmitters has not been deciphered, and so it is not understood how thoughts or feelings are processed through chemical and electrical processes. In reality, the neurosciences have not provided us with a general theory as to how neural circuits function, how mental or behavioral states are generated, or how mental imbalances are produced. So far, the study of neurons has failed, resulting in a need to broaden the research horizon (e.g., by studying sets of neurons rather than the operation of each single neuron).

It is very likely that the model of neuronal transmissions is incomplete or even wrong. This is precisely the claim of the physicist Thomas Heimburg, whose research on biological membranes, with a thermodynamic focus, has led him to state that the propagation of nerve pulsations cannot be explained by the electrochemical processes, based on the former Hodgkin-Huxley model, established more than seventy years ago. Heimburg sustains that the nerve signals are propagated through mechanical pulsations in the form of waves, like the so-called solitons, those solitary waves that are propagated in nonlinear media for long distances without changing. The transmission of signals in the nerve membranes would more likely be an electromechanical phenomenon.[1] I do not know whether the cerebral keys to thinking can be found by that route or if the signals that travel through the central nervous system can be deciphered. But this new interpretation is possibly a symptom that the neuronal paradigm has reached a dead end.

In contrast to the scant knowledge about the transmission of signals in the nervous system, engineers understand the functioning of the "brains" of robots very well, because they have designed them and built them. But at present, how intelligent machines could develop a symbolic system that would enable them to perform functions and operations that their electrical brain cannot is not known. In fact, the builders of robots do not have a universally accepted general theory of the cognitive system, so they must explore alternatives, based on different interpretations. My reflections stem from the theory I have developed on the exocerebrum, but few robot designers have proposed programming the operative system of their machines to include a complex symbolic environment that serves as a support and a prosthesis. I am thinking of robots endowed with an entirely new system that is neither a copy of the human brain nor a structure similar to the neural networks. The other option would be to upload the content of a brain onto a computer, a purely imaginary solution, given that not only do we not yet have the technology to do so, but also, as I have said, scientists do not know how brain activity generates the mind. It is not possible to copy or upload the content of a brain if we do not understand the system of signals it operates with.

For now, it is preferable to start from robots and systems that actually exist and to speculate on how they could develop an artificial consciousness. If the brain of a robot, like those Jun Tani has described, contains a nonlinear dynamic system, such as a strange attractor, it must be capable of understanding and processing the symbols of its environment, in addition to moving about without bumping into walls, as well as having the capacity to target specific goals. These symbols are what at present drive and enlighten the humans who are part of the robot's environment. Engineers must find a way in which they can merge numerical signs and symbolic codes into their system. To do so, robots must have a broad and flexible intelligence that is not very specialized, capable of dealing with multiple tasks.

This problem cannot be properly confronted if it is based on the idea, so generalized today, that the same mathematical rules that apply to human organisms apply to electronic machines as well. The point of departure is often the erroneous idea that all organisms function through algorithms and that animal activities (including those of humans) are regulated by data-processing mechanisms. As I have already described, electronic computers and biological brains do not share algorithms that regulate flows and information encoded through mathematical or logical signs.

We are up against a problem similar to the question faced in physics: the macroscopic world does not function by the same rules as the microscopic world. The latter is governed by the probabilistic quantum theory, whereas the former functions with the classic Newtonian laws of physics. But in reality, the two worlds coincide in a confluence of two spheres, the biological world of the brain and the symbolic world of the exocerebrum. The first operates through mechanical, electrical, and chemical processes, and the second functions through a symbolic system of a cultural and social nature. Reducing one world to the norms of the other does not allow the phenomenon of consciousness to be understood. But here we find ourselves in a situation worse than that of the physicists. Quantum mechanics is well understood and has decidedly been the driving force behind the modern electronics industry. What physicists do not understand is the time at which the two worlds touch, so to speak, and the occurrence of what Werner Heisenberg calls a "collapse." That takes place the instant a human measures a wave, an act that happens before the particle "chooses" a position or state. No one understands why the conscious human intervention causes the quantic overlap to disappear. The theory explains what *could* happen but not the mechanics of how the probable turns into the real. The quantic collapse has generated other interpretations, such as the idea of continuous spontaneous location (CSL), in which the collapse occurs randomly. The loss of coherence has also been seen as an explanation of the collapse. Another interpretation suggests that there is no collapse or decoherence, but rather all possibilities are real and coexist in a multiverse. I have already referred to the paradox of Schrödinger's cat to exemplify the way in which physics introduces the theme of human consciousness into quantum theory.

When the cerebral world comes into contact with the cultural world there is a kind of "collapse," and those aspects that function according to deterministic biological laws have social, political, and economic consequences governed by very different rules. A most important difference between the two sets of rules is that there is no such thing as free will in the biological universe, but the instant it connects with the cultural world there is a "collapse," because free will, as a capacity characteristic of humans, suddenly emerges. An easy way to escape from this paradox is to proclaim that humans do not have a unique ego capable of deciding and choosing. Free will would be a myth. This evasion allows us to close our eyes to the fact that human consciousness is a phenomenon that eludes traditional scientific determinism.

Would it be possible for engineers to connect the brain of robots to an external system—one that is symbolic in nature and does not function through mathematic algorithms? The experiment could be carried out, following two paths. The more remote route is the organization of a society of interconnected robots capable of autonomously generating a network of symbolic cultural, institutional, and conventional links. Such an alternative requires the design of robots with a highly developed general intelligence, something that is still very far off. The second option is to connect intelligent robots (albeit still specialized) to the social and cultural networks of humans. This second alternative is something that extensively occurs on a daily basis in environments with advanced technological development, where humans are surrounded by robots that help them with many diverse tasks, calling to mind the various personal assistants, such as Siri from Apple, Cortana from Microsoft, Bixby from Samsung, or Assistant from Google. However, these systems do not have even the tiniest spark of consciousness. In reality, they are more like prostheses that prolong human consciousness, the way smartphones and the different translation programs or GPS guides for drivers do. Automatic cars with no drivers are also very useful prostheses, but when one of them crashed and killed a pedestrian in Arizona in March 2018, it did not appear to show any conscious remorse.

If we shift our attention to the world of art, where robots have long intervened, we can observe creations of immense beauty and originality. Jean Tinguely, the great precursor of robotic art, wanted, as he said, "to make truly joyful machines, and by joyful, I mean happy." His Métamatics are robots that draw abstract works by means of an electric motor that moves both the paperboard and the arm holding the pen. In 1959 his *Métamatic No. 17* amazed the public at the Paris Biennale by producing some forty thousand works in a few days, each of them different and very attractive. I do not think this machine was happy, and its apparent freedom was the product of random mechanical movements, but it definitely produced great joy in those that witnessed the spectacle of the primitive robot artist.

Earlier, in 1956, Nicolas Schöffer built the CYSP 1 machine, which was the first cybernetic sculpture in the history of the arts. The sculpture contains an electronic brain connected to light and sound receptors. The machine reacts to external stimuli, and consequently moves sixteen polychrome plates that spin at different speeds. It undoubtedly produces an aesthetic pleasure in the spectators.

An especially interesting example is provided by the artist Patrick Tresset, who in 2004 began to create robots he utilized to draw people's portraits in a very peculiar and attractive style. Initially, Tresset drew the portraits himself, but a mental illness—bipolar disorder—profoundly affected his life. The drugs he took to control his manic-depressive oscillations made him lose his passion for art. Rather than suspending his medications and living as a prisoner to bipolarity, he decided to apply his computational abilities to a robot named Paul, which had an eye and arm capable of drawing in a style similar to his own. Tresset actually created a prosthesis endowed with a certain autonomy that draws portraits with a peculiar crudeness, or in his words, "clumsy robotics."

In recent years, dozens of robotic artists have been created that produce impressive work. An exhibit at the Grand Palais in Paris, *Artistes & Robots* (2018), presented a very good selection of machines and works, revealing the expansion of a new and very provocative field of artistic experimentation. However, the works of these machines have not overcome a paradox: the creations of these robots thrill us and awaken very diverse feelings, but the robots are as cold as a block of ice.

17 SENTIMENTAL MACHINES

I believe the technological singularity needed to create an artificial consciousness is still very far off. However, for the intelligent and ingenious posthumanist prophet Ray Kurzweil, the first indications of the "Singularity" will be seen by the year 2045.[1] To predict such an imminent outcome, Kurzweil does not base it on current technical achievements but rather on a proposed "law of accelerating returns," according to which the discoveries in research would grow at a fabulous, exponential rate. At this accelerated speed of technical and scientific advances, the Singularity should emerge right away, even though no one knows from where. The presumedly rapid growth of artificial intelligence will result in machines making it possible for us to free ourselves from the biological body. Of course, just like the engineers responsible for creating artificial intelligence systems, Kurzweil believes that the human brain and machines share algorithms and computational mechanisms that will be the basis for this singular leap. Marvin Minsky, one of the founders of artificial intelligence, had already expressed such a view: "The brain is merely a meat machine." Hence, transferring or copying the mental content of the human brain onto a computer is thought to be possible.

To explore this seemingly fantastic dimension, I wish to travel to a far distant future, with the help of a beautiful text published in 1988 by Jean-François Lyotard.[2] The French philosopher stated that the only truly serious problem facing humanity has no relation to wars, conflicts, political tensions, changes of opinion, philosophical debates, or passions. For Lyotard, the greatest problem is the fact that the Sun is aging, and within some 4.5 billion years it will explode, destroying all traces of our planetary system and life on Earth.[3] Humanity's only escape, according to him, will be to find the way to simulate the conditions that make thinking materially possible when the conditions that sustain life on Earth have disappeared. The solution is to manufacture a hardware capable of "nourishing" a software as complex as the present-day human brain. This is precisely what the builders of artificial intelligence systems and robots propose to do. But human thinking does not function in a binary manner or with information bits: it operates analogically, not logically. The challenge is to create something better than a poor binarized ghost of what used to be the brain.

Lyotard adds one more problem that is much more troubling: the fact that thinking and suffering overlap. The hues in painting, tones in composing music, or the words and phrases in writing are given to us, but at the same time they slip through our fingers. All of these aspects of art "say" something different from what we actually want to "mean," forming a part of an opaque world, full of emptiness, that produces suffering. Remember that thinking must be inscribed in culture. Lyotard wonders whether thinking machines will suffer or will only have memories. I would add that, in addition to suffering, thinking is accompanied by pleasure and other emotions.

A fundamental dimension that worries Lyotard is rarely taken into account by those dedicated to artificial intelligence. The human body manifests differences with respect to sex and gender. The philosopher believes that there is an incompleteness, not only in bodies, but also in minds. The incompleteness of femininity and masculinity is not only corporeal but also resides in thinking. An attempt is made to overcome this incompletion through attraction, thanks to the powerful force of desire. Lyotard wonders whether the intelligence that is prepared to survive the solar explosion would include this inner force on its interstellar journey. Thinking machines will have to be nourished, not only by radiation, but also by the irremediable discrepancy of gender. Post-solar thought must be prepared to face the inevitability and complexity of sexual difference and separation if it is to survive the threat of entropy.

Some will say that because humanity is so young—barely one hundred thousand years old—the more than four billion years we still have left will be more than enough time to invent a technical alternative that frees us from the earthly body that depends on solar light, taking us on a cosmic journey to new conditions of existence. However, the need to detach ourselves from the body could arrive before the solar explosion, if, for example, a malignant mutation of a virus forces humans to move their thinking away from the biological support that has housed it from the very beginning.

Such a futuristic thought experiment is quite a disturbing science fiction, distant but also stimulating. Nevertheless, the problems posited by Lyotard are real: the builders of artificial intelligence systems face the challenge of introducing the enigma of feelings and the phenomenon of sexuality into their programs and machines. But these very difficult problems are rarely addressed.

The idea of sensitive machines has been widely explored in science fiction and is generally expressed in the form of a technique capable of uploading the mind housed in the brain onto a computer. It is the dream of the transhumanists, whose aspiration is for humans to be freed from their soft and humid support, placing flesh aside, to be inserted into a hard and dry mechanism that does not require any biological process in order to obtain energy. Of course, despite their dryness and hardness, the tendency is to imagine emotional machines that would be capable of experiencing pleasure and suffering, thanks to the sensitivity that makes us human and simultaneously connects us with the rest of the animals.

Some transhumanists wear a medallion around their neck that is reminiscent of those pendants or amulets the physician Qusta ibn Luqa was interested in. This medallion identifies the wearer as a member of a cryogenic institution dedicated to maintaining cadavers at very low temperatures in order to revive them when a method for curing the disease that killed them has been discovered, or in the hope that one day there will be a technology capable of copying the dead brain and uploading the information onto a computer. The medallion contains the inscription, not of a spell, but of the precise instructions for treating the body, in case of death, and sending it to the institution that will keep it frozen for centuries. In some cases, only the head is frozen, with the expectation that one day the content of the brain can be downloaded onto a machine that will give the person a new cybernetic life. The singularity enabling this operation does not appear to be close at hand, but it is undoubtedly an alternative to the challenge Lyotard describes: to achieve this feat, humanity has a long time before the solar system disappears within those 4.5 billion years. It is very likely that the singular downloading of a consciousness onto a machine can only be done with living beings; thus the bodies that frozenly await their resurrection will not fulfill the hopes of the transhumanists who opted for cryogenics.

It seems to me that intelligent machines will not reach the point of having a consciousness similar to that of humans without possessing some kinds of sensations, feelings, and emotions. An artificial intelligence system, whether its consciousness comes from a downloaded brain of a human or has been constructed from a new design, will not be able to function at a human level if it lacks feelings. To face the challenge posited by Lyotard, these intelligent and sensitive consciousnesses must be mounted on nonorganic supports populating huge space machines, perhaps circulating in orbits similar to those of a comet. But a problem not contemplated by Lyotard would potentially arise: given their metallic structure, these beings imbued with artificial consciousness could be immortal, or live many centuries or millennia, signifying a leap that would essentially modify human nature.

And so, dear readers, leaving you to now continue imagining such a future on your own, I shall return to the theme of the sensitivity of robotic machines. How can engineers introduce emotions and sexuality into intelligent robots so they can obtain an artificial consciousness, similar to that of humans? I have already cited the idea of the physicist Max Tegmark, who imagines a substance called *sentronium*. But that gives us no specific idea about how such a substance capable of having subjective experiences can be elaborated or how it can appear. *Sentronium* would be like a wave or an algorithm that is independent of its specific physical substrate. For now this idea is as useless as thinking a robot could acquire feelings by way of a divine breath. The majority of speculations on the future of artificial intelligence are based on the supposition that this divine breath (or Singularity, as they prefer to call it) is something that will occur sooner than later.

I have insinuated above that a reversal could take place that ends up converting humans into prostheses of the superintelligent machines. Humans will be the *sentronium* of a robot. This new human condition could end in the nightmare of converting us into mere pieces of meat, in charge of transmitting sensations and feelings to powerful machines much more intelligent than humans. Perhaps we can feel and imagine this new condition if we recall the experience of the use of cognitive devices that support, increase, and even substitute human perceptions. There are many, such as those that create virtual reality and simulated environments. Some are games and others are systems for learning or observation. Flight simulators, as games or as pilot training systems, are a good example of the articulation of a being of flesh and blood with an intelligent virtual reality. Anyone who has tried out these simulators can imagine that, suddenly, the machine turns them into its sensitive prostheses. When we connect to Second Life, a game that has created an intelligent virtual reality in which humans are introduced through avatars, we can apparently inject our emotions and desires into an artificial environment. We have become a conscious and feeling piece of meat, plugged into an artificial world by means of a computer. Some intelligent cybernetic systems increase our perceptions, such as the devices that register dimensions unperceived by the driver of a car or the pilot of an airplane. Other systems of augmented reality are the combination of a virtual environment with a real one. Several games, through screens, helmets, and visors, create experiences that mix perceived reality with virtual elements.

These games are very far from the singular divine breath that will make robots conscious. But there are futurologists who have imagined social life after the breath that would have caused the multiplication of conscious robots. The projection an economist makes of a future in which the entire workforce has been substituted by robots is significant. Robin Hanson, in his book *The Age of Em,* explains that in about one hundred years, in the twenty-second century, all human workers will have been replaced by a first version of robots, built from emulations of the complete brain of living persons. From this supposition, he attempts to illustrate the resulting social and economic world.[4] It is a world in which humans no longer work and robots called ems (emulations) sustain the economy. An em is the result of the copying of all the neurons of a given human brain, and the connections that unite them, to then construct a computational system capable of processing signals, according to the characteristics copied. The outcome is an em that behaves very similarly to the original, so much so that humans can speak to the machine and convince (or force) it to do useful jobs. These ems reside in their own cities, away from the places where humans live a comfortable life, enjoying the investments they have made in the robot economy. The robots, on the other hand, organize in clans that group the descendants of the same original brain together. The ems are sexed beings that can be happy, sad, tired, have hopes and fears, make friends, and have lovers. The immense majority of the ems, more than 80 percent, live a digital and virtual life in the circuits of computers, and only those that perform physical work have bodies. But their bodies have no resemblance to the bodies of humans. Hanson supposes that these androids will be tiny (265 times smaller than a human) but much faster, both physically and mentally. It is symptomatic that in this version of the future, robots appear that have emotions and feelings. Actually, they could be efficient systems lacking sensitivity, but Hanson has wanted to add a bit of emotion to his technocratic and boring version of that kind of digital world imagined by Philip K. Dick in his disquieting novels. The reader of Hanson's book will search in vain for an explanation as to how humans have been able to build intelligent and sensitive robots that work for them.

The building of robotic systems capable of using a sophisticated language model, the so-called LLM (large language model), has already begun. The LLM is a statistical system that has learned to predict the words that are more likely to appear together. By injecting or feeding a massive amount of text into the model's algorithms (called deep neural networks), the system learns complex linguistic patterns. The model does this by playing: it randomly takes a text, hides a certain number of words, and then tries to recompose the text, filling in the gaps. Humans rate the results of the statistical process to train the system to predict the missing words and formulate fluid, coherent phrases, resulting in systems such as the famous ChatGPT, which I have referred to above. Interestingly, things occur in these models that their own creators do not understand; they do not really know what goes on inside them when they manifest emergent abilities they were not trained to have. Apparently, these systems develop a kind of understanding of the world that goes beyond the purely statistical process their inventors created for them.[5] Nevertheless, there is not even a hint that they have developed a sensitivity similar to that of humans.

18 PROOF OF THE PLACEBO

We will be in the presence of a truly conscious robot the moment we prove that it experiences relief from some type of malaise, by giving it a placebo. Such a response will be the necessary proof that the machine possesses a system that can be tricked and, as a result, stops feeling sick. Even though I have expressed many doubts about the way intelligent machines endowed with consciousness could actually be built, I am convinced that this endeavor will succeed, but not as quickly as some would hope. The creation of robots with consciousness will not be achieved until a very complex problem is solved: how to assemble in a single system a nonspecialized, broad-spectrum artificial intelligence that has some form of nonorganic life, is capable of self-organization and self-replication, and possesses sensitivity. The cybernetic and mechanical equivalents of a signal-based brain will have to function within such a system, together with an exocerebrum supported by cultural symbols.

The construction of a general intelligence comes up against very complicated technical problems. The first step will be to combine several specialized systems that can agilely coordinate with each other. Such a feat will require enormous computational strength and capacity—currently nonexistent—but will someday be achieved through the evolution of technology. Perhaps the perfecting of quantum computers will change this panorama. The construction of a robot with a general, broad, flexible intelligence, capable of adapting to and operating in unstructured, unknown environments, can be put into practice only through a machine that is capable of learning. A truly intelligent robot must learn by observing what humans (or other robots) do, or through trial and error. The so-called deep learning, as I have already pointed out, is advancing in this direction, but it is still very far from reaching a general capacity for multifaceted learning.

The elaboration of nonorganic life-forms is a much more tangled and difficult problem. I believe that to advance in this terrain it is necessary to abandon the very fixed idea that consciousness is separate from the material substrate that processes it. The forms of consciousness we presently know have a biological substrate that provides sensitivity, enabling them to exist at a higher level. In fact, without a sensitive biological substrate there can be no primary forms of consciousness, such as those of a mouse, a cat, or a dolphin. This leads me to contemplate the possibility of creating nonorganic life-forms, but forms whose initial transitional phase could involve robots connected to a synthetic organic material. This material would provide the machine with the necessary sensitivity for sustaining conscious processes similar to those of humans. I like the idea of artificial biological cultures that are capable of transmitting pain, pleasure, and other sensations to a powerful machine that possesses a general intelligence. This alternative is not so technologically far from reality, given that there has already been some success in the creation of artificially designed organs, grown in animals or in laboratories. Designing an interface that can connect them to a machine, as well as transmit sensations, will be more complicated.

Now, if we think of superintelligent robots endowed with consciousness that do not depend on the conditions we know on Earth and have the capacity to survive a post-solar condition such as the one Lyotard imagined, then it would be necessary to build artificial, nonorganic life-forms capable of organizing autonomously and possessing sensitivity. Serious thought and experimental trials are already rudimentarily pointing toward this alternative. Manuel DeLanda, for instance, has studied nonorganic self-organizing phenomena that occur with the appearance of what physicists call "bifurcations."[1] There have also been efforts to create a kind of metallic life with polyoxometalates. But we are a long way from seeing the construction of complex forms of metallic life. All known organisms utilize carbon compounds as the basis of metabolic and structural functions. Alternative life-forms based on metalloids, such as silicon, are a mere speculation.

The problems facing the creation of an artificial consciousness revolve around something I have implicitly assumed but now wish to directly address. From my perspective, a conscious machine must constitute an individuality. Consciousness involves the definition of a sensitive ego that is perceived as different from other consciousnesses it lives with, as well as relatively separate from the environment surrounding it. But regarding the construction of intelligent machines, there are those who have thought of the possibility of robots endowed with a collective intelligence, similar to that which presumedly exists in a hive. The internet has been used as an example of a supposed collective consciousness that functions like an insect colony. A kind of communal soul is assumed to exist in such colonies, with each insect lacking individuality. I do not know whether such a collective spirit exists in animal societies, but I am convinced that if a network of collectively functioning robots were to be built, there would not be a higher form of consciousness unless limits were defined separating that network from others. In such a case, the conditions for an individual consciousness would emerge, a robotic ego, a self-consciousness. This idea clashes with the supposition that consciousness is an illusion that does not comprise a unit. For example, the well-known scholar of cognitive phenomena Francisco Varela stated that a centralized and unitary ego does not exist. He believed that Buddhism is correct in affirming that the ego is a chimera, empty of all substantiality. For Varela, the ego lacks identity and is nothing more than an apparent, overall pattern that emerges from the activity of simple components that appear to be centrally located but are nowhere to be found.[2] The philosopher John Gray has enthusiastically embraced these ideas and supposes that humans are not made of one single piece: they are a succession of fragments. The ego is a fiction, an illusion.[3] This idea is so deeply rooted that it has disrupted, and even stopped, research on the biological and cultural bases of consciousness. Applied to artificial intelligence, this interpretation considers that a robot is nothing more than a collection of competing behaviors that lack a central system and are only a unit in the external eyes of an observer. This is the conclusion of Rodney A. Brooks, a renowned specialist in robotics and information technology.[4] These ideas are a product of the vision of one of the founders of artificial intelligence, Marvin Minsky, who popularized the theory of the "society of mind," according to which the human mind is composed of several hierarchically organized autonomous agents that are specialized and interconnected and deprived of intelligence.

I am more inclined to strongly emphasize the role of homeostasis as an essential biological fact for understanding consciousness, as the neurologist Antonio Damasio has expressed in all his books. At the elemental level of a bacterium, as well as in the functioning of the human body, homeostasis involves the capacity to regulate the inner environment, consequently keeping it stable, balanced, and separate from the outer environment. A conscious robot must have the sensitivity necessary for maintaining a homogeneous and stable inner environment, which necessarily involves the formation of an individual system. Consciousness requires a sensitivity capable of distinguishing the interior environment from the exterior one. Robots tend to be defined as "autonomous agents" capable of detecting their environment and acting according to their own agenda, and as such they are individual systems that possess an identity.

But the theme of individual identity places us in front of a singular paradox. Human consciousness generates an individual identity because it extends beyond the limits of the body, thanks to an exocerebrum composed of symbolic artificial prostheses. The mechanisms of homeostasis cannot be rigidly applied, because of a singularity: to define the ego, consciousness must expand toward the others that are in our environment. Human consciousness needs to maintain an internal environment that is simultaneously an external one, because the brain perceives the intrusion of exogenous elements that are artificial in nature. Thus it is useful to understand that there is another process that complements homeostasis and enables a certain balance to be maintained in the face of the heterogeneity appearing in the networks of consciousness due to its hybrid character. While homeostasis maintains the interior environment balanced around a "normal" point, heterostasis changes that point of equilibrium when, for example, the organism finds itself in the presence of toxic exogenous substances. This triggers a process of tolerance of the external agents, with which it establishes a new balance, and occurs when the organism has to adapt to high levels of poisonous contaminants, drugs, or alcohol. Tolerance increases in the presence of toxins, and a dependency appears. As I explained in my book *Anthropology of the Brain,* the symbolic and instrumental prostheses have developed thanks to a dependency of the brain, which in addition to becoming addicted to them also adapts to the new situations, because it establishes a new balance with the artificial part of its environment. Hence, heterostasis is what induces, in humans, what I have called a *sociodependence* of the cerebral circuits, caused by their incompleteness.[5]

I am convinced that a robotic consciousness will come up against this same problem. To consolidate its conscious identity, it will have to open and extend its internal circuits in such a way as to generate an interaction between the cybernetic system and the cultural environment of the machine. If robots accomplish that, android individuals with inclinations that are difficult to foresee could appear. Perhaps the experiment would spawn strange monsters that would then need to be annihilated, or to the contrary, creative beings could emerge that would be beneficial company for the humans of the future. Science fiction has been nurtured by these possibilities and has produced very attractive myths. If the construction of intelligent and conscious robots is finally successful, there will surely be a certain autonomy and their evolution could become a threat. These androids would be capable of replicating or reproducing themselves. The emergence of a wide variety of conscious robots, the result of different technologies associated with the groups or companies that created them, would not be surprising. But we are facing different kinds of artificial beings, with different capacities. We would have machines marked by their origin, characterized by a dangerous primal inequality. We could say that the original sin of these robots would be the design with which they were built, marking them forever. The different brands of robots would be surrounded by different exocerebral subcultures and form something like tribal groups, possessing peculiar and distinctive symbolic hives.

My imagination is flying too far away, but with this flight to an unknown future I have wanted to stress the importance of the exocerebral circuits in the construction of intelligent robots. Conscious machines cannot be built in the absence of symbolic, social, and cultural environments. It is possible that the engineers creating the robots of the future connect them to the same exocerebral circuits used by humans, which would attenuate the disparities imprinted in each brand or type of conscious machine. This theme leads us directly to the problem of robot ownership, because when all is said and done, they would be artifacts built by companies, laboratories, and manufacturing plants. But, by being conscious and, in turn, having will, these mechanical machines cannot be treated simply as slaves and the servants of those who have built them or bought them. Faced with this problem, there are those who believe it would be more prudent to abandon the efforts to create artificial consciousnesses. I am not convinced that is the most sensible thing to do, and I am certain that the research directed at endeavoring to construct artificial consciousnesses will not be stopped.

The impulses leading to the creation of conscious robots seek another similar achievement: that of changing the biological support structure of human consciousnesses, to install it in the machinery of a robot. This is a path parallel to the construction of autonomous machines with their own robotic consciousness, but here an attempt would be made to create cybernetic artifacts that house the minds that abandoned their biological body in order for them to migrate to a much longer mechanical existence. We can suppose that this radical change of substrate would also involve a profound transformation of consciousness as we presently know it, and I suspect that these beings would end up resembling completely artificial androids. Important inequalities could also be produced in this context, caused by the differences in the kinds of mechanical support that each person would have been able to acquire.

For robots to attain forms of consciousness as sophisticated as those of humans, and not be insensitive zombies, they must pass through the rituals of pleasure and pain. Without the suffering of distress and without the pleasure of its alleviation, it is difficult to conceive of intelligent humanoid machines guided by a developed and complex consciousness. The healing lies of the placebo effect are part of an extensive and ramified culture that encourages illusions, myths, and pleasures—a culture that includes threats, frustrations, and deceptions, and that is not unconnected to the magic of power. In the end, robots will be conscious if a shaman of the future is able to captivate them, through adeptly wielding the art of the word, and their sensitivity to the placebo effect is proven.

NOTES

Prologue

1. Roger Bartra, *Anthropology of the Brain: Consciousness, Culture, and Free Will*, trans. Gusti Gould (Cambridge, UK: Cambridge University Press, 2014).

1. The Placebo

1. Sigmund Freud, *Beyond the Pleasure Principle,* trans. C. J. M. Hubback (London: International Psycho-Analytical Press, 1922).

2. The Ligatures of Qusta ibn Luqa

1. The Melkites were Christians from Syria, Egypt, and Palestine, loyal to the Byzantine emperor (Malka, in Syrian). The Melkite churches originally had their own ritual but ended up adopting the Byzantine ritual.
2. Giuseppe Gabrieli, *Nota bibliografica su Qusṭā ibn Lūqā* (Rome: Reale Accademia dei Lincei, 1912).
3. I use the Latin transcription and the English translation by Judith Wilcox and John M. Riddle in their study "Qusṭā ibn Lūqā's Physical Ligatures and the Recognition of the Placebo Effect," *Medieval Encounters* 1, no. 1 (1995): 1–50.

4. Most certainly the translator to Latin substituted Scotland for Scythia. The Hippocratic texts make references to the Scythians.
5. The term *epōidós* (epode) was used by Homer to refer to words that have a therapeutic effect. The *Charmides* deals with an incantation or charm. An epode is the last verse of a strophe, repeated many times, and in Greek poetry was the third part of a lyric ode (strophe, antistrophe, and epode).

3. The Magical Powers

1. See Manuel Durán's reflections on shamanism: Manuel Duran, "On Shamans, Magic, and the Birth of Poetry," *Antemnae* (Rome, 2001): 39–58.
2. V. M. Mikhailovskii, "Shamanism in Siberia and European Russia," *Journal of the Anthropological Institute of Great Britain and Ireland* 24 (1895): 62–100. It is a translation of the original, published in 1892 in volume 12 of the acts of the Ethnography Section of the Russian Imperial Society of Natural History, Anthropology and Ethnography. Sergei Mikhailovich Shirokogoroff, *Psychomental Complex of the Tungus* (London: Kegan Paul, 1935).
3. Jean-Paul Roux, "Turkish and Mongolian Shamanism," *Mythologies,* comp. Yves Bonnefoy (Chicago: University of Chicago Press, 1991).
4. Claude Lévi-Strauss "The Effectiveness of Symbols," in *Structural Anthropology,* trans. Claire Jacobson and Brooke Grundfest Schoepf (New York: Basic Books, 1963), 201.
5. Ernesto de Martino, *Primitive Magic: The Psychic Powers of Shamans and Sorcerers* (Dorset: Prism Press, 1990).
6. De Martino, 125.
7. Croce's "Intorno al 'magismo' come età storica," originally published in *Filosofia e storiografia* (1949), is included in de Martino, *Primitive Magic*, 279–91.
8. Eliade's "Science et phénomènes paranormaux" is also found in de Martino, *Primitive Magic*. See Eliade's classic book *Shamanism: Archaic Techniques of Ecstasy,* trans. Willard R. Trask (Princeton: Princeton University Press, 1964).

9. Wilfred Barbrooke Grubb, *An Unknown People in an Unknown Land: An Account of the Life and Customs of the Lengua Indians of the Paraguayan Chaco, with Adventures and Experiences during Twenty Years' Pioneering and Exploration amongst Them* (London: Seeley, Service, 1913).
10. Lucien Lévy-Bruhl, *Primitive Mentality*, trans. Lilian A. Clare (Boston: Beacon Press, 1923), chapter 3, "The seen and unseen world form one," 98.
11. Lucien Lévy-Bruhl, *The Notebooks on Primitive Mentality,* trans. Peter Rivière (Oxford: Blackwell, 1975), 100–101.
12. David Gordon Wilson, *Redefining Shamanisms: Spiritualist Mediums and Other Traditional Shamans as Apprenticeship Outcomes* (London: Bloomsbury, 2013). The perspective of a non-indigenous shaman from the United States can also be consulted in the encyclopedia prepared by Christina Pratt, *An Encyclopedia of Shamanism* (New York: Rosen, 2007). Pratt is the head of the Last Mask Center for Shamanic Healing in Portland, Oregon.

4. A Shamanic Journey in Search of the Lost Soul

1. I do not use Lévi-Strauss's 1947 translation but rather the complete 1953 version: Nils M. Holmer and S. Henry Wassén, *The Complete Mu-Igala in Picture Writing: A Native Record of a Cuna Indian Medicine Song* (Stockholm: Etnografiska Museet, 1953).
2. Apparently the child is on the verge of coming out or has already come out, but the placenta is not expelled. That is the interpretation of Staffan Mjönes, "Shaman, Psychoanalyst or Obstetrician: A Critical Reading of Claude Lévi-Strauss' Essay 'The Efficiency of Symbols,'" *Folklore* 45 (August 2010): 7–26.
3. Lévi-Strauss was only familiar with the chant up to this point because the last part was not published in the edition he consulted. For the new edition of his essay he did not take the trouble to consult the complete 1953 version. He mistakenly believed that the delivery had already taken place, even though it was not described in the Kuna text he knew. He also was unaware of the pictographic version. As explained by Mjönes, the woman had not yet expelled

the placenta and its retention was probably the cause of her affliction.
4. Michel Perrin, "Between Representations, Knowledge and Practice: The Art of Shamans and Other Traditional Practitioners," *IRD Éditions,* 2002.
5. Michael Taussig, *Shamanism, Colonialism, and the Wild Man: A Study in Terror and Healing* (Chicago: University of Chicago Press, 1991), 389–92.
6. Marguerite Sechehaye, *Autobiography of a Schizophrenic Girl,* trans. Grace Rubin-Rabson (New York: Grune & Stratton, 1951).

5. Neurology of the Placebo Effect

1. Fabrizio Benedetti, Elisa Carlino, and Antonella Pollo, "How Placebos Change the Patient's Brain," *Neuropsychopharmacology* 36 (2011): 339–54.
2. See Henry K. Beecher, "The Powerful Placebo," *Journal of the American Medical Association* 159 (1955): 1602–6.
3. Anne Harrington, *The Cure Within: A History of Mind-Body Medicine* (New York: Norton, 2008).
4. Benedetti, Carlino, and Pollo, "How Placebos Change the Patient's Brain," 348.
5. Benedetti, Carlino, and Pollo, 349–50.
6. Oron Frenkel, "A Phenomenology of the 'Placebo Effect': Taking Meaning from the Mind to the Body," *Journal of Medicine and Philosophy* 33 (2008): 58–79.
7. Jennifer Jo Thompson, Cheryl Ritenbaugh, and Mark Nichter, "Reconsidering the Placebo Response from a Broad Anthropological Perspective," *Culture, Medicine and Psychiatry* 33 (2009): 112–52.
8. Daniel E. Moerman, *Meaning, Medicine, and the "Placebo" Effect* (Cambridge, UK: Cambridge University Press, 2002).
9. Franklin G. Miller, Luana Colloca, and Ted J. Kaptchuk, "The Placebo Effect: Illness and Interpersonal Healing," *Perspectives in Biology and Medicine* 52, no. 4 (2009): 1–20.
10. Fabrizio Benedetti, "Placebo and the New Physiology of the

Doctor-Patient Relationship," *Physiological Reviews* 93 (2013): 1207–46.

11. Irving Kirsch, "Antidepressants and the Placebo Effect," *Zeitschrift für Psychologie* 222, no. 3 (2014): 128–34.

12. Pim Cuijpers and Ioana A. Cristea, "What If a Placebo Effect Explained All the Activity of Depression Treatments?," *World Psychiatry* 14, no. 3 (2015): 310–11.

13. Fabricio Benedetti and Aziz Shaibani, "Nocebo Effects: More Investigation Is Needed," *Expert Opinion on Drug Safety* 17, no. 6 (May 2018): 541–43.

14. J. D. Levine, N. C. Gordon, and H. L. Fields, "The Mechanism of the Placebo Effect," *The Lancet* 312, no. 8091 (September 23, 1978): 654–57; Fabrizio Benedetti, Helen S. Mayberg, Tor D. Wagner, Christian S. Stohler, and Jon-Kar Zubierta, "Neurobiological Mechanisms of the Placebo Effect," *Journal of Neuroscience* 25 (2005): 10390–10402.

15. Jonathan J. Lipman, Barney E. Miller, Kit S. Mays, Merry N. Miller, William C. North, and William L. Byrne, "Peak B Endorphin Concentration in Cerebrospinal Fluid: Reduced in Chronic Pain Patients and Increased during the Placebo Response," *Psychopharmacology* 102 (1990): 112–16.

16. Alina Dumitriu and Bogdan O. Popescu, "Placebo Effects in Neurological Diseases," *Journal of Medicine and Life* 3, no. 2 (2010): 114–21.

17. Fabrizio Benedetti, "Drugs and Placebos: What's the Difference?," *EMBO Reports* 15, no. 4 (2014): 329–32.

18. Rasha Al-Lamee et al., "Percutaneous Coronary Intervention in Stable Angina (ORBITA): A Double-Blind, Randomised Controlled Trial," *The Lancet* 391, no. 10115 (January 6, 2018): 31–40.

19. There is a good general description with many examples in the previously cited books of Moerman and Harrington. Alain Autret's *Les effets placebo: Des relations entre croyances et médecines* (Paris: L'Harmattan, 2013) offers an excellent general perspective.

20. Antonio Damasio, *The Feeling of What Happens: Body and Emotion in the Making of Consciousness* (New York: Harcourt Brace),

51 and 60. See also Antonio Damasio, *The Strange Order of Things: Life, Feeling, and the Making of Culture* (New York: Pantheon, 2018).

6. On Electronic Amulets and Catharsis

1. On the nocebo effect, see A. Tinnermann, S. Geuter, C. Sprenger, J. Finsterbusch, and C. Büchel, "Interactions between Brain and Spinal Cord Mediate Value Effects in Nocebo Hyperalgesia," *Science* 6359 (October 6, 2017): 105-8.
2. Russell W. Belk, "Possessions and the Extended Self," *Journal of Consumer Research* 15 (1988): 139-68.
3. Russell B. Clayton, Glenn Leshner, and Anthony Almond, "The Extended iSelf: The Impact of iPhone Separation on Cognition, Emotion, and Physiology," *Journal of Mediated Communication* 20 (2015): 119-35.
4. Dan-Mikael Ellingsen, Johan Wessberg, Marie Eikemo, Jaquette Liljencrantz, Tor Endestad, Håkan Olausson, and Siri Leknos, "Placebo Improves Pleasure and Pain through Opposite Modulation on Sensory Processing," *PNAS* 110 (2013): 17993-98.
5. Sigmund Freud, "Psychical (or Mental) Treatment," in *The Standard Edition of the Complete Psychological Works of Sigmund Freud,* vol. 7 (London: Hogarth Press, 1953-74), 281.
6. Sigmund Freud, "On Psychotherapy," in *The Standard Edition of the Complete Psychological Works of Sigmund Freud,* vol. 7 (London: Hogarth Press, 1953-74), 259.
7. Freud, 266-67.

7. Zombies and Transhumanists

1. Stevan Harnad, "Why and How We Are Not Zombies," *Journal of Consciousness Studies* 1 (1995):164-67.
2. Augustine of Hippo, *The City of God,* 14:23:3.
3. Gerald Edelman, *Wider Than the Sky: The Phenomenal Gift of Consciousness* (New Haven: Yale University Press, 2004), 80, 145, and 180.
4. Ray Kurzweil, *The Singularity Is Near: When Humans Transcend*

Biology (New York: Viking, 2005). See Mark O'Connell's entertaining and ironic examination of transhumanism, *To Be a Machine: Adventures among Cyborgs, Utopians, Hackers, and the Futurists Solving the Modest Problem of Death* (London: Granta, 2007).

8. The Mystery of Thinking Machines

1. Susan Blackmore, "Consciousness in Meme Machines," in "Machine Consciousness," ed. Owen Holland, special issue, *Journal of Consciousness Studies* 10, nos. 4-5 (2003): 19-30.
2. Susan Blackmore, *Conversations on Consciousness: What the Best Minds Think about the Brain, Free Will, and What It Means to Be Human* (Oxford: Oxford University Press, 2006), 203.
3. Peter Farleigh, "The Ensemble and the Single Mind: A Sceptical Inquiry," in *Artificial Consciousness,* ed. Antonio Chella and Riccardo Manzotti (Exeter: Imprint Academic, 2007), 256-76.
4. See Roger Penrose, *The Emperor's New Mind* (Oxford: Oxford University Press, 1989).

9. The Robotic Effect

1. See Alan Winfield, *Robotics: A Very Short Introduction* (Oxford: Oxford University Press, 2012), 8. A good general introduction to robotics is Laurence Devillers, *Des robots et des hommes: Mythes, fantasmes et réalité* (Paris: Plon, 2017).
2. Winfield, *Robotics*, 51-54.
3. See Stan Franklin, "IDA: A Conscious Artifact?," in "Machine Consciousness," ed. Owen Holland, special issue, *Journal of Consciousness Studies* 10, nos. 4-5 (2003): 77-109.
4. Franklin, 64.
5. Winfield, *Robotics,* 132.
6. Vincenzo Tagliasco, "Artificial Consciousness: A Technological Discipline," in *Artificial Consciousness,* ed. Antonio Chella and Riccardo Manzotti (Exeter: Imprint Academic, 2007), 12-23.
7. Murray Shanahan, *The Technological Singularity* (Cambridge: MIT Press, 2018).

10. How Do You Educate a Robot?

1. The reader can see how DeepMind functions at https://tinyurl.com/atariai.
2. Apurv Mishra, "AI That Sees Like Humans," *Scientific American* 317, no. 6 (December 2017): 33.
3. Murray Shanahan, *The Technological Singularity* (Cambridge: MIT Press, 2018), 3.
4. Terrence J. Sejnowski, *The Deep Learning Revolution* (Cambridge: MIT Press, 2018).
5. There is a good overview of artificial intelligence in Margaret A. Boden's book *AI: Its Nature and Future* (Oxford: Oxford University Press, 2016).

11. Panpsychism

1. Max Tegmark, *Life 3.0: Being Human in the Age of Artificial Intelligence,* 300–305. I critique Tononi's theses in *Anthropology of the Brain: Consciousness, Culture, and Free Will*, trans. Gusti Gould (Cambridge, UK: Cambridge University Press, 2014), 143–45.
2. Christof Koch, *Consciousness: Confessions of a Romantic Reductionist* (Cambridge: MIT Press, 2012), 118.
3. Koch, 311.
4. Michio Kaku, *The Future of the Mind: The Scientific Quest to Understand, Enhance, and Empower the Mind* (New York: Doubleday, 2014), 334.

12. A Mechanical Consciousness

1. Murray Shanahan, *The Technological Singularity* (Cambridge: MIT Press, 2018), 6–10.

13. Robotic Culture

1. See Jerry Fodor, *The Language of Thought* (Cambridge, Mass.: Harvard University Press, 1975). A general overview of the idea that the mind is a machine and of the computational theory of cognition see Tim Crane, *The Mechanical Mind. A Philosophical Intro-*

duction to Minds, Machines and Mental Representation, 3rd ed. (London: Routledge, 2016).
2. The irony of Marx appears in the last chapter of the first volume of *Das Kapital,* dedicated to the modern theories of colonization, and is based on what the great exponent of the "art of colonization," Edward Gibbon Wakefield, relates.

14. Prostheses and Symbols

1. Murray Shanahan, *The Technological Singularity* (Cambridge: MIT Press, 2018), 122–25.
2. Michael S. A. Graziano, "The Attention Schema Theory: A Foundation for Engineering Artificial Consciousness," *Frontiers in Robotics and AI* 4 (November 2017). See also his book *Consciousness and the Social Brain* (Oxford: Oxford University Press, 2013).

15. Robotic Experiences

1. Jun Tani, *Exploring Robotic Minds: Actions, Symbols, and Consciousness as Self-Organizing Dynamic Phenomena* (Oxford: Oxford University Press, 2017).

16. Emancipation of the Exocerebrums

1. See Thomas Heimburg, "Phase Transitions in Biological Membranes," *arXiv.org:* 1805.11481v1, 2018, and Thomas Heimburg and Andrew J. Jackson, "On Soliton Propagation in Biomembranes and Nerves," *PNAS* 102, no. 28 (2005): 9790–95. And the stimulating commentary on soliton communication by Douglas Fox, "The Brain, Reimagined," *Scientific American* 318, no. 4 (2018): 53–59. Other studies posit similar theses, such as those by Ahmed El Hady and Benjamin B. Machta, "Mechanical Surface Waves Accompany Action Potential Propagation," *Nature Communications* 6, no. 6697 (2015), http://doi.org/10.1038/ncomms7697.

17. Sentimental Machines

1. Ray Kurzweil, *The Singularity Is Near: When Humans Transcend Biology* (New York: Viking, 2005), chapter 3.

2. Jean-François Lyotard, "Can Thought Go On without a Body?," trans. Bruce Boone and Lee Hildreth, Discourse 11, no. 1 (Fall-Winter 1988-89): 74-87. This text is based on a session he gave at a seminar held at the German University of Siegen, invited by Hans Ulrich Gumbrecht.
3. Astronomers currently believe the solar system will still last six or seven billion years, or even more.
4. Robin Hanson, *The Age of Em: Work, Love, and Life when Robots Rule the Earth* (Oxford: Oxford University Press, 2018).
5. George Musser, "An AI Mystery," *Scientific American* 329, no. 2 (September 2023): 58-61.

18. Proof of the Placebo

1. Manuel DeLanda, "Nonorganic Life," in *Zone 6: Incorporations*, ed. Jonathan Crary and Sanford Kwinter (New York: Urzone, 1992), 128-67.
2. Francisco J. Varela, *Ethical Know-How: Action, Wisdom, and Cognition* (Stanford: Stanford University Press, 1999).
3. John Gray, *Straw Dogs: Thoughts on Humans and Other Animals* (New York: Farrar, Strauss and Giroux, 2002).
4. Rodney A. Brooks, "Achieving Artificial Intelligence through Building Robots," *A.I. Memo 899* (Massachusetts Institute of Technology Artificial Intelligence Laboratory, May 1986).
5. Roger Bartra, *Anthropology of the Brain: Consciousness, Culture, and Free Will,* trans. Gusti Gould (Cambridge, UK: Cambridge University Press, 2014), 178-81.

ROGER BARTRA is a Mexican anthropologist recognized as one of the most important contemporary social scientists in Latin America. He is the author of many books, including *Anthropology of the Brain: Consciousness, Culture, and Free Will*; *Angels in Mourning: Sublime Madness, Ennui, and Melancholy in Modern Thought*; and *Melancholy and Culture: Diseases of the Soul in Golden Age Spain*.

GUSTI GOULD is an artist and translator in Colima, Mexico.